MYSTERY AND TERROR
The Story of Edgar Allan Poe

MYSTERY AND TERROR
The Story of Edgar Allan Poe

William Schoell

MORGAN
REYNOLDS
Publishing, Inc.

620 South Elm Street, Suite 223
Greensboro, North Carolina 27406
http://www.morganreynolds.com

MYSTERY AND TERROR: THE STORY OF EDGAR ALLAN POE

Library of Congress Cataloging-in-Publication Data

Schoell, William.
  Mystery and Terror : The Story of Edgar Allan Poe / William Schoell.
    p. cm.
  Includes bibliographical references and index.
  ISBN 1-931798-39-7 (library binding)
  1. Poe, Edgar Allan, 1809-1849—Juvenile literature. 2. Authors, American=
—19th century—Biography—Juvenile literature. I. Title.
  PS2631.S36 2004
  818'.309—dc22

                    2004008356

Printed in the United States of America
First Edition

Sandra Cisneros

Virginia Woolf

Edgar Allan Poe

Jane Addams

Isak Dinesen

H.P. Lovecraft

Gwendolyn Brooks

Richard Wright

Henry Wadsworth Longfellow

Nathaniel Hawthorne

Stephen Crane

F. Scott Fitzgerald

Langston Hughes

Washington Irving

Edgar Rice Burroughs

H.G. Wells

Sir Arthur Conan Doyle

Isaac Asimov

Bram Stoker

Mary Shelley

Jules Verne

Ida Tarbell

George Orwell

Mary Wollstonecraft

World Writers

Contents

Edgar Allan Poe (1809-1849)
(Photo by John Miller, Brown University Library.)

Chapter One

Fall From Grace

Trying to forge a career in the theater made for a hard life in the early nineteenth century. Working on the stage meant traveling in wagons and carriages on terrible roads. It meant living in poor, sometimes unsanitary conditions, often in close proximity to members of the opposite sex who were not necessarily family members. It meant working long nights in smoke-filled theaters before audiences that may or may not show any sign of appreciation or respect.

Today, actors are hailed as celebrities. Adoring fans follow them in search of their autographs, and photographers earn thousands of dollars for taking their pictures. But in the nineteenth century, many proper, hard-working, church-going Americans thought the theater was a den of iniquity that distracted one from church, work, and family. To these upstanding citizens, people who made their living in the theater were disreputable.

There was also little chance that working in the theater

Eliza Arnold Poe. *(Rare Book Department, Free Library of Philadelphia.)*

would make the actors and actresses wealthy. It was often a family trade. Children who grew up watching their parents perform nightly would often grow up to become actors themselves, just as the children of farmers became farmers and the children of silversmiths became silversmiths. As the century developed, some acting families did gain a measure of respect and a bit of renown. The Booth family, for example, produced several famous actors, including one who assassinated a president. The Barrymore family first began acting in the nineteenth century and continued producing actors well into the twentieth.

Eliza Arnold was an actress who was born into a lesser-known British family of thespians. She emigrated with her family to Boston when she was nine and soon after took up the family trade. Along with her family, Eliza performed in plays up and down the East Coast. She was eighteen years old and performing in Richmond, Virginia when she met a handsome young actor, three years her senior, named David Poe. After being cast together as lovers in a number of plays, real life merged with their stage roles. They married in 1806 and continued their careers. Though the couple called Boston home, they continued to travel frequently, scratching out a living performing melodramas and tragedies.

David Poe was different from most actors because he came from a prosperous and respected family. His family had disowned him when he insisted on going onto the stage, and his background had not prepared him for the challenging life he had chosen. Performers were usually given only a day or two to learn their parts, and most memorized literally hundreds of characters over the course of their careers. It was a stressful existence and it was not uncommon for many to turn to drink to alleviate the pressure. Matters were made more difficult for the newlyweds because Eliza was more successful and popular than her husband. They often fought about money, a problem made worse by the birth of two sons in two years' time. William Henry Leonard Poe was born in 1807 and his brother Edgar in 1809.

When little Edgar was six months old, the Poes moved to New York City, where they hoped to find better roles at the prestigious Park Street Theater. But the pattern that bedeviled them in Boston continued in the new city: Eliza's performances were generally well reviewed, and David Poe remained unpopular with audiences. Critics even made jokes about him in the newspapers. Humiliated and frustrated, he began drinking heavily, and finally, one day, he disappeared without a trace. His family never saw him again.

Left to raise two children alone, Eliza Poe struggled financially. Sympathetic theater friends held benefit performances, but there was never enough money. She took her boys with her when she toured the southern states in 1810, and while in Virginia, Eliza gave birth to a third child, a daughter she named Rosalie. The father of that baby is unknown.

A few months after Rosalie's birth, Eliza became ill. She took to bed with a high fever and had to rely on the kindness of others to care for and feed her children. David's family in Baltimore was contacted, but they refused to send money or help in any way. Eliza lingered near death for nearly a year before expiring, at the age of twenty-four, on December 8, 1811.

Eliza's three children now had neither father nor mother. Neighbors took in Rosalie, the youngest, while William's paternal grandparents in Baltimore grudgingly took him in. Frances Allan, called Fanny, one of the women who had cared for Eliza while she was dying, wanted to take Edgar. Fanny had been an orphan herself and felt sorry for the little boy. The Poes and the Arnolds were happy to have one less mouth to feed. Edgar Poe went to live with

John and Fanny Allan.

John Allan was, at thirty-two, a successful merchant in the burgeoning town of Richmond. He had emigrated from Scotland to America at the age of sixteen. His uncle, William Galt, had given the young man a job as a clerk in his tobacco firm. Allan resented what he thought was unfair treatment from his uncle, and after only five years he formed a company called the

Fanny Allan, Edgar's surrogate mother. *(Edgar Allan Poe Museum of the Poe Foundation, Richmond, Virginia.)*

House of Allan and Ellis with a friend, Charles Ellis. The company sold a wide variety of goods: everything from tobacco and plaster of Paris to coffeepots and frying pans.

For the rest of his life, Allan would harbor bitterness and resentment towards his uncle William Galt. Though the older man did try to help his nephew, Allan would always maintain he had not done enough. Because he thought his uncle had made his life more difficult than it had to be, all his life Allan insisted he was a self-made man. He had no patience with idlers or people who could not look after themselves. He was a firm believer in personal responsibility. When he discovered he had an illegitimate son, he immediately acknowledged the child and provided the mother with monetary support.

Edgar was three years old when he entered the Allan household. The Allans were prosperous and lived in a nice home with servants. Edgar's life there was comfortable. Twenty-six-year-old Fanny Allan coddled the little boy, happy to have a child in the house. She was a kind woman who suffered from both real and imagined illnesses. John Allan worried that his wife was not up to the stress of caring for a child, but little Edgar took Fanny's mind off of her own worries and fears. In general, Edgar's early years were uneventful. He played with other children, including a little neighbor that he thought of as his girlfriend. He came down with the usual childhood illnesses, attended Sunday school, and was well liked by the headmaster at his regular school.

When Edgar was six, in 1815, the Allans moved to England. The House of Allan and Ellis was expanding to London, and John went to oversee the opening of the new office. It was an arduous thirty-four-day trip across the Atlantic. Their quarters were cramped, and John let Fanny and Edgar have the tiny bed while he slept on the floor every night of the journey. Many people were seasick, and dangerous weather made everyone fear for their survival.

Once safely across the ocean, John took his family to meet the relatives he had left behind in Scotland. From there they went to London and rented a furnished home complete with a house-keeper. After some initial difficulties, fortunes improved for the London House of Allan and Ellis and the firm prospered. John Allan liked being a successful businessman in a big British city. He decided to extend their stay beyond the planned two years and moved the family into larger quarters. He also arranged for Edgar to go to school.

John Allan. *(Edgar Allan Poe Museum of the Poe Foundation, Richmond, Virginia.)*

Arrangements were made for Edgar, now seven, to go to Scotland to live with John Allan's relatives and begin his schooling. A teenage cousin named James was sent to bring the boy from London. Young Edgar proved to be an unpleasant traveling companion—he complained the whole trip, begging to be returned to Fanny and John in London. Even after James managed to get the boy to Scotland, Edgar continued to be difficult. He spent most of his time sulking. It was impossible to teach him anything. He kept threatening to make his way back to England by himself. James had to sleep in the same room at night to keep him from carrying through on his threat.

Finally, the Allans told John they could not keep the unhappy boy any longer. Edgar was delighted to learn he was going back to London, but crushed when he found out he was being sent to a boarding school in Chelsea, several miles away from the Allans' London quarters. Edgar never understood why he had to be separated from his newfound family, and in later years was bitter over the situation. He remembered feeling lonely and isolated.

John and Fanny visited Edgar on the weekends, but John was preoccupied by business concerns and Fanny by worry over her own health. Before long John Allan had more serious problems: the main item sold by the London House of Allan and Ellis was tobacco, and in 1819 the bottom dropped out of the London tobacco market. One competing firm went bankrupt, and Allan and Ellis was itself on the brink of collapse. John appealed to the main office in Virginia for help and cash, but they were having trouble of their own. State banks in America were rapidly failing, causing the ruin of many businesses.

By the summer of 1819, the precarious situation worsened. The London House of Allan and Ellis could no longer afford to pay its employees or pay off its mounting debt, which was nearly a quarter of a million dollars. John Allan could no longer even pay his own rent, and had little money to give to Fanny to buy food. Ellis sent Allan enough money to keep his family from starving, and John negotiated with his creditors for more time to settle his debts. It was time for the penniless Allan family to return to America.

Back in Richmond, the Allans could not afford a place of their own, so they boarded with the Ellis family for a while. For the next two years they moved around from place to place. Finally, around 1823, John's uncle William Galt gave them the loan of a house in the warehouse district. It was quite a comedown from their previous standard of living, but Fanny summoned up a measure of strength that bolstered John and helped him get through this trying period. John and Charles Ellis managed to pay off half of their company's debt by selling off valuable real estate holdings, but ultimately had to declare bankruptcy. John's uncle acquired the firm's assets and tried to help his nephew by making him a secret partner.

Edgar was now fourteen and attending the Clarke Academy, where he studied math, science, English, and French with twenty or so other male students. He developed an interest in Latin poetry, particularly the works of Horace and Cicero. By age sixteen he was writing his own poetry, including a satire entitled "Oh, Temporar! Oh, Morcs!" about a clerk in a dry goods establishment. It was probably no accident that Edgar chose a merchant as the target of his withering contempt—he and his guardian were having trouble getting along.

Edgar, according to those who knew him best, was already developing an aggressive and overbearing personality. He was undeniably talented as a poet. But when he asked John Allan to pay to have his work published in book form, Joseph Clarke, who ran the academy where Edgar studied, told Allan it would be a mistake to do so. Clarke worried that Edgar was already haughty and that it would do too much for his ego if he became a published author at such a young age.

Despite this disappointment, Edgar continued to try out new literary forms. He also began experimenting with romantic feelings, developing an obsessive infatuation with Jane Stannard, the kindly thirty-year-old mother of a classmate. Fanny Allan's precarious health prevented her from giving Edgar the maternal attention he needed and Jane Stannard filled that void. But Jane was also ill, suffering from severe depression and emotional instability. Within a year of Edgar's meeting her, she died, insane.

Both Jane's and Fanny's illnesses affected Poe deeply. Many of the stories he went on to write contain people suffering from mental conditions they are powerless to overcome. At that time, many people believed that mental illness was the result of defective character and could be cured if the patient would only try hard enough. In contrast, Poe's personal experiences convinced him that mental illness was a part of a person, something an individual could not control but was, instead, controlled by. He was fascinated by people who lived outside the bounds of normal society and did not—or could not—behave the way most others did.

Edgar reveled in athletic competition. He loved to run, box, and most of all, swim. Despite his slight build, he was strong and eager to take on any challenge. He tended to be the boss in his group of friends, which included Thomas Ellis, whose father was John Allan's business partner. Edgar instructed Thomas in shooting and skating, among other sports. At sixteen, Edgar garnered attention and admiration from peers and locals by swimming six miles in the James River against the current. Thomas Ellis was among the band of boys who accompanied him in a boat as he proceeded steadily up the river. With this act, Poe was emulating the Romantic poet Lord Byron, who, in his youth, swam the Hellespont (the strait that connects the Agean and the Sea of Marmara and separates the European portion of Turkey from the Asian). Byron, in his turn, had been emulating Leander, a hero of Greek mythology who supposedly swam across the Hellespont to make clandestine visits with his lover. Poe, like Byron, was intrigued by broad, if ultimately useless, romantic gestures.

In 1824 Edgar became a lieutenant in the Junior Morgan Riflemen and rode with them in a procession when the Marquis de Lafayette visited Richmond in October. Lafayette had known Edgar's grandfather, General David Poe, during the American Revolution. He related the story of how the man had managed to raise money to buy desperately needed clothing for the soldiers. Edgar was thrilled to be personally reviewed in his uniform by Lafayette, and to hear stories praising his ancestors.

Young Edgar may have had considerable self-esteem, but there was one thing that bothered him deeply—John and Fanny Allan had never legally adopted him. Much of Edgar's bluster and brash behavior came from the desire to be seen as better than his peers, to prove he was worthy of being made an addition to any family. He also sought comfort in stories about the celebrity of his ancestors— General David Poe, and Edgar's own mother, Eliza Poe, who some people still remembered for her fleeting fame

John Allan bought Moldavia, the family home, with inherited money in 1825. *(The Valentine Museum, Richmond, Virginia.)*

as an actress. Uncertain about his place in the Allan household, Edgar developed a bold personality to cover his insecurity.

As for the rest of his family, Edgar only saw his siblings on occasion. William Henry Leonard came to Richmond to visit Edgar once or twice, and the two managed to form a bond that lasted until William's early death. Rosalie was sickly and frail in her youth and though she lived nearby, Edgar saw her only a few times.

For many years Rosalie believed she was the natural child of the family that had adopted her. One of their relatives ran a school for young ladies and it was there where Rosalie spent most of her time. Edgar saw more of Rosalie during his final years but the two were never close.

In March of 1825, the fortunes of the Allans took a dramatic turn for the better when William Galt passed away while eating breakfast. He was one of the richest men in Virginia, owning plantations, sawmills, bank stock, hundreds of slaves, and a great deal of property. John Allan's share of the inheritance, which included several estates, as well as the house his family was living in, was valued at seven hundred fifty thousand dollars.

Within a couple of months, John had used some of his inheritance to buy an estate called Moldavia. It consisted of a two-story brick house with its own ballroom, an octagonal dining room, several smaller outbuildings, and a variety of flourishing gardens. Edgar was given his own bedroom on the second floor, but he was still not given the permanent place in the family that might have alleviated some of his fears and insecurities.

Chapter Two

Battle of Wills

In February of 1826, Edgar enrolled in the University of Virginia in Charlottesville. Founded by Thomas Jefferson in 1819, the university consisted of eight schools, each headed by a prominent professor. One hundred seventy-seven students attended the university. Located near the Blue Ridge Mountains, the school's buildings had been constructed along classical lines—the library, for instance, was modeled on the Pantheon in Rome.

Though it was customary for students to enroll in three schools within the university, Edgar signed up only for two: the School of Ancient Languages and the School of Modern Languages. John Allan had given him a certain amount of money but it was not enough for Edgar to enroll in three schools and pay for his books, clothes, and lodging as well. This began a flurry of letters between the two men—John Allan accused Edgar of being lazy and greedy, while Edgar argued he could not possibly be expected to make do on the paltry sums John Allan begrudged him. The University of Virginia was one of the most expensive in the country and catered mostly to the sons of wealthy families.

For much of his life, Edgar Poe struggled with feelings of inadequacy combined with the conviction that he was smarter and more talented than the people around him. These contradictory emotions had one thing in common: Poe's fervent belief· that if he had enough money, his problems would go away. For Poe, money equaled security. If he had money of his own, he would not have to worry about John Allan's approval. If he had money of his own, his peers would respect him instead of mocking him. If he had money of his own, he could feel comfortable and safe. Unfortunately, he would never have money of his own.

John Allan's considerable inheritance from William Galt fueled Edgar's anger and jealousy. He believed that if only John Allan had adopted him, he would have a right to some of that money. He wrote many letters to Allan, alternately begging and demanding further financial support. Allan, convinced the young man should make ends meet on his own, steadfastly refused to send aid.

Edgar compensated for his feelings of inadequacy and inferiority by spending money freely, even hiring a man-servant to tend to his needs. He wrote to Allan that in order to afford even the basic necessities, he had had to take up gambling. But Edgar was not a successful gambler and was soon deeply in debt. He compounded this debt by borrowing money from his wealthier classmates, insisting again that he needed the money for living ex-

This famous rotunda at the University of Virginia was designed by Thomas Jefferson. *(The Cook Collection.)*

penses. When John Allan expressed his disappointment in the young man, Poe blamed the people around him and his own loneliness for his behavior: "I call God to witness that I have never loved dissipation—Those who know me know that my pursuits and habits are very far from any thing of the kind. But I was drawn into it by my companions. Even their professions of friendship—hollow as they were—were a relief."

Unmoved, Allan pointed out that the items Edgar bought on credit and which contributed to his debt were not necessities for his education or room and board, but fancy waistcoats and vests and other items of clothing he wore to impress his friends. Allan's implacability only made Edgar more defensive, and the two continued to argue about money.

Edgar did well in his studies, especially Latin and French, and continued his athletic pursuits with the same spirit of competitiveness as before. When several classmates achieved a running broad jump of nineteen feet, Edgar did them one better by jumping twenty. He also continued to write poetry and sometimes etched charcoal drawings for the amusement of himself and his friends.

At seventeen, Edgar was two years younger than the average student, which increased his sense of isolation. The university was a wild, rough place for a young man. Jefferson did not believe in the strict discipline found at the established Ivy League schools. Students could govern themselves, Jefferson felt, without being bogged down by excessive rules.

This radical approach not only led to numerous fights and assaults, public drunkenness, and outrageous conduct such as the theft of test papers, but there was once a full-fledged riot in which the students hurled bottles and books at their professors. Many of the students carried guns, and there were several near-fatal incidents involving firearms. Things only quieted down a bit when the faculty demanded that the students be subject to more traditional discipline and rules of behavior.

When he was not studying or engaging in extracurricular activities—or dodging fists, bullets, or bottles—Poe was writing letters to a girl he had met back in Richmond, shortly before leaving for Charlottesville. Her name was Elmira Royster. Elmira was fifteen and found Edgar to be shy and quiet, but very pleasant. Elmira's father was adamantly opposed to an older boy courting his daughter so he made sure that none of Edgar's letters to Elmira reached her. Edgar agonized over the fact that she never wrote him back, which only increased his loneliness at school.

After his first year at the university, Edgar returned to Richmond, bringing with him debts of nearly twenty-five hundred dollars. John Allan was furious. He not only refused to pay off the debts, but he refused to allow Edgar to return to Charlottesville for another term. Edgar was not as upset about leaving school as he was that Allan would not bail him out. Nearly every day a classmate, creditor, or even a law official would arrive at the Allan home demanding payment for one debt or another, and John turned them all away. In those days people could be imprisoned for failing to pay money they owed. Only Edgar's youth prevented him from being hauled off to jail.

Adding to Edgar's emotional turmoil was the fact that he was not allowed to see his sweetheart, Elmira Royster. Her father kept the couple apart by telling Edgar first that she had become engaged to someone else, and later, that she had been shipped off to some relatives.

Tension between John Allan and Edgar reached the

boiling point, and the two men nearly came to blows over Edgar's debts and behavior. In a fit of pique, Edgar announced he was moving out. "My determination," Edgar wrote Allan, "is at length taken—to leave your house and indeavor [sic] to find some place in this wide world, where I will be treated—not as *you* have treated me." Later, Edgar would say John Allan had ordered him out of the house. Though it is impossible to know exactly what transpired that summer, it is clear that John Allan did not try to stop Edgar from leaving, and that Edgar felt the sting of rejection for many years to come. His belief that John Allan did not value him as a son had been confirmed.

Edgar stayed with friends for a while and spent most of his time at the Courthouse Tavern, where his mail was being forwarded. He occupied himself writing angry letters to John Allan, who he accused of thwarting his chances of attaining an education and ever amounting to anything in life. "You take delight in exposing me before those whom you think likely to advance my interest in this world," Poe wrote. It is easy to see the hurt and pain in Poe's many letters to his guardian, and to see his desire for reconciliation in the many chances that he gave Allan to offer it.

Allan did not take the bait. At first, he only replied sternly that Edgar was sabotaging his own chances for success by wasting his time reading and writing all day. John Allan believed Edgar needed to take responsibility for himself and get his life together, and he was particularly annoyed by what he saw as Edgar's greediness.

Edgar would send letters lodging dozens of complaints and asserting his need to live his own life—and then would beg for money in a postscript. In one letter, Edgar claimed that he was penniless, had nowhere to sleep, was hardly eating, and would not ask for anything if the situation had not been so desperate. Then he asked for twelve dollars so that he could make his way to Boston, the city of his birth, where he might make a fresh start. Disgusted, John Allan sent the letter back to Edgar with no money and no reply.

John Allan was right when he suspected that Edgar Poe was not making much of an effort to find a job. Instead, Edgar was busy trying to outwit his creditors. Since his brother, William Henry, had gone off to sea, Edgar adopted Henry's adventures in South America and elsewhere as his own. Running into friends or associates of John Allan, he would tell them he would be shortly setting sail for some distant port. At other times Poe masqueraded as a Frenchman, Henri Le Rennet. Using these methods he managed to confuse and elude the people he owed money. After a time, even John Allan assumed that he had gone off to sea like his brother.

In truth, Edgar had left Richmond, but not for South America. Instead, he went north to Boston where he hoped to find spiritual replenishment and a new life brimming with success. He managed to find work in a business similar to the House of Allan and Ellis before switching to a newspaper office. He wrote copiously in his spare time and somehow saved up enough money to have a small booklet of his poems printed. (As the printer was around Edgar's age and his family had known Edgar's actor parents, he may have printed Edgar's poems for free or at a reduced rate.) The resulting booklet was entitled *Tamerlane and Other Poems*. Its author was simply listed as "a Bostonian." Though he craved recognition of his talent, Edgar also feared being discovered by his creditors.

The title poem is written from the point of view of the Mongol conqueror Tamerlane (also known as Timur) as he dies and confesses his sins. Tamerlane is thought to have slaughtered tens of thousands of people during his invasions of Persia and India. Edgar was probably more attracted to the historical figure because he was also known as a patron of the arts. The nine other poems all have to do in some fashion with pivotal events in the speaker's childhood that led to his feelings of alienation in adulthood. They reflect the adolescent Edgar's sadness and anger at his sorry lot. *Tamerlane and Other Poems* received no reviews and did not make much of an impression on the Boston literary scene.

After a dissolute and disappointing year trying to scrape by, Edgar decided to enlist in the United States Army. At least in the army he would be fed. His grandfather's military background may also have been in the back of his mind. Giving his name as Edgar Perry, he enlisted in late May of 1827 for a five-year term.

Edgar was one of thirty-nine privates in the First Regiment of Artillery, which was stationed at Fort Independence near Boston harbor. Over the next few months his regiment moved several times, first to South Carolina, and later to Fort Monroe on the Chesapeake Bay in Virginia. Life in the army was not unpleasant. Edgar had no problem following orders and eventually became an assistant commissary in charge of the food supply— ensuring that he would always be well fed if nothing else.

Based on his performance in the commissary, Edgar was also given the duties of company clerk, which made him responsible for writing up numerous reports each month. He managed to find time for his own writing, and got along well with the other privates and officers. Army life seemed to suit him—he certainly did not find it difficult or especially challenging—and eventually he was awarded the rank of sergeant major. As a non-commissioned officer, he could go no higher.

While Edgar felt safe and comfortable in the army, he was also monumentally bored. He felt as if he was stagnating, as if life was passing him by. After two years he decided he wanted to leave. He hoped he would be discharged if army officials discovered that he had en-listed under a false name. He confessed everything to a kindly officer named Lieutenant Howard, who was sym-pathetic but reminded Edgar that, fake identity or not, he had pledged a five-year commitment. Knowing young Poe was impulsive and excitable, Howard wrote to the boy's guardian for advice.

Edgar's angry remarks in previous letters and his seeming ingratitude, not to mention the hordes of Poe's creditors still hovering near the Allan home, all rankled John Allan. He told Howard that it would be better if Edgar stayed in the army for the full term; it might teach him some responsibility. Even when Edgar himself wrote to him, begging to be released from his commitment, Allan remained unmoved. After several unanswered letters, Edgar tried a new tactic. He wrote to John Allan saying that he had decided upon a military career. Rather than asking for Allan's help to get out of the army, he asked John Allan to use his influence to help him secure an appointment to the United States Military Academy at West Point.

Edgar also decided it would be politic to withdraw his earlier accusations and blame only himself for the debts he had incurred at school. He wrote John Allan that he had lost his head because he had never before been away from home or Allan, who he called his guiding influence, for so long a period. Edgar's flattery may have worked if he had not added a postscript to the letter asking for money.

In the end, it was tragedy that brought John and Edgar back together. Fanny Allan was very ill, and begged John to bring Edgar home for a visit. She was wasting away from a lingering and difficult disease—probably cancer.

Edgar was able to get compassionate leave from the army to visit Fanny, but he arrived too late. He appeared at Moldavia only to learn that she had died and been buried the night before. Edgar was nearly as upset as John Allan was at her death. He felt enormous guilt at not having seen Fanny for over two years.

Worn down by grief, Allan bought Edgar some clothes and told him he would support him in his plan to enter West Point and would do what he could to help him. Alone again, Edgar headed back north.

Chapter Three

West Point

Before Poe could leave the army for West Point, he needed to find someone to take his place in his regiment. He found a man who would do so for the price of twelve dollars, and Poe was discharged in April of 1829. Lieutenant Howard and other officers gave Poe letters of recommendation. John Allan wrote on Edgar's behalf to Secretary of War John Eaton, who reviewed all West Point applications and related material. In his letter John Allan took pains to make it clear that Edgar was not related to him, but only someone he wanted to help. Eaton must have found the discrepancy between Allan's letter and Poe's application interesting.

On his application Poe had rewritten his family history. He claimed that both of his parents had been killed in the infamous Richmond Theater Fire that had occurred two years before his mother's death. He wrote that he had been adopted by John Allan and was his heir. It is possible that John Eaton understood Poe's reasons for lying and did not hold the fabrications against him, or perhaps Edgar made changes on the application before submitting it. In any case, Eaton wrote to Edgar to say that his was the eleventh name on the waiting list for West Point. As weeks went by, John Allan, disturbed by the delay, accused Edgar of only pretending to desire entry to the academy. Edgar assured him this was not the case—there was nothing he could do to put his name farther up on the waiting list—and suggested that Allan himself should be working harder to help him. Old resentments and bitterness began to resurface, and before long, Edgar and John Allan were arguing about money again.

Since leaving the army, Poe had been living in Baltimore, where he stayed in a hotel with a cousin named Edward Mosher. John Allan had reluctantly sent Poe one hundred dollars—twelve of which was supposed to go to the man taking his place in the Army. The rest was for Poe's living expenses while he waited to be summoned north. But Mosher stole forty of Edgar's dollars, and Edgar wrote to John Allan saying that he had used the other fifty to pay his Army substitute. Now, he said, through no fault of his own, he needed more money. Allan wrote back, angrily, accusing Edgar of lying—why would he have given the soldier fifty dollars when the originally agreed upon sum was twelve? Though Edgar did not stop asking, Allan refused to send more cash.

Poe did not spend his time in Baltimore idly. He kept busy introducing himself to prominent men in Baltimore and Philadelphia who might be useful to him. These included William Wirt, the former Attorney General of the United States, and the editor of the *American Quarterly Review,* Robert Walsh. He approached these men with flattery, then asked them to read his work. Encouraged by their positive remarks about his latest lengthy poem, "Al Aaraaf," he submitted it to the Philadelphia publishing house of Carey, Lea, and Carey.

Taking his cues from the Koran (the sacred book of Islam) and contemporary astronomy, Poe created in his poem a purgatory (known as "Al Aaraaf" in the Koran) which he situated in an actual distant star, a nova that had been discovered in 1572. There, those who were neither saints nor terrible sinners, including many famous people, waited for admittance to Heaven. The poem is very long and today is not considered Poe's best work.

During this period, most writers self-published their books, paying the printing cost themselves and keeping any profits. Edgar did not have the money to pay for his poem to be printed, so he asked John Allan to subsidize it. By subsidizing the printing, Allan would agree to pay the publishers for any copies of the poem that went unsold. Edgar was positive "Al Aaraaf" would make money, but John Allan was not. Still suspicious of Edgar's intentions regarding West Point, and annoyed at the way he ran through his money, Allan refused to help. Predictably, Carey, Lea, and Carey then rejected "Al Aaraaf."

Edgar did find a publisher for "Al Aaraaf" in the Baltimore firm of Hatch and Dunning. The seventy-one-page-long publication was entitled *Al Aaraaf, Tamerlane, and Minor Poems,* and the author was billed as Edgar A.

Poe. Although Poe is now known universally as Edgar Allan Poe, throughout his lifetime he was known professionally as "Edgar A. Poe." John Allan never formally adopted him and the two had a complicated relationship, but Poe used Allan as his middle name to honor Fanny.

After its release, *Al Aaraaf* was reviewed in some important publications. In general it was held that Poe demonstrated a prodigious talent, but that the poem was too often obscure. Despite its rich and powerful use of language, many critics found Poe's longer work too rough and amateurish in spots. His shorter poems met with better reception.

Edgar Poe was finally accepted into West Point in March of 1830. In the months between his receipt of the acceptance letter and his actual entrance into the academy in June, he stayed with John Allan at Moldavia. It seemed impossible for the two men to be in close quarters without all the old tensions rising up and leading them into their bitter disputes.

Allan found out that the sergeant who had taken Edgar's place in the army had received not fifty dollars, as Poe had claimed, but was still waiting for the twelve he had agreed to accept. Allan accused Edgar of lying and being up to his old irresponsible tricks. In his anger, Allan implied that Edgar could not be expected to be honest since he came from a family of actors. This slur wounded Poe deeply. In retaliation, he wrote to the sergeant who replaced him in the army, complaining that although he had tried many times to get the money he owed him from John Allan, the latter kept sloughing him off. Still smarting from his arguments with Allan, he added with impudence that Allan was generally drunk. News of this letter got back to Allan, who became enraged and convinced that Edgar was a complete ingrate. After Edgar left for West Point, Allan sent him a letter accusing him of taking books and other things that did not belong to him. Edgar responded haughtily that he had only taken what was his. These petty quarrels would persist for years.

West Point Military Academy is located along the Hudson River, about fifty miles from New York City. Although there were several sets of barracks at the academy, in the summer the new cadets shared tents on the grounds. During the day, Edgar and his fellow cadets practiced drills, studied for tests, and learned the proper way to clean, load, and shoot various firearms. The cadets rose at five and went to bed at nine-thirty. When cold weather came, they transferred from the tents to indoor barracks.

In the fall the cadets began their classes. Edgar studied French and mathematics. At this time the policy at West Point was for cadets to become highly proficient in just a few subjects instead of becoming mediocre in many. Edgar excelled at both his subjects, although at first he was a bit perturbed at the sheer number of hours he spent each day studying.

Edgar was well liked by most of his teachers and fellow cadets. He amused them by using his vivid imagination to tell marvelous tales. He also invented outlandish stories about his own past. He created for himself an exciting life, distinguished by his singular bravery and

Two West Point cadets relaxing outside their summer encampment. *(United States Military Archives.)*

resourcefulness. He claimed to have had incredible adventures sailing to South America, to be the grandson of the notorious traitor Benedict Arnold, and to have run away in his youth from a horrible man who had adopted him.

After feeling like an outsider at the University of Virginia and even in the Allan household, Poe wanted to fit in. He was sensitive to the fact that he was several years older than most of the other cadets and was not amused when a story circulated that the real Edgar Poe had died and his own father had taken his place at West

Point. But Poe overcame this ribbing, and found that he loved West Point. He finally felt as though he was part of a genuine, caring family. He needed a new family; John Allan had remarried and wanted nothing more to do with him.

Allan's new wife was thirty-one-year-old Louise Patterson, a lawyer's daughter who was twenty years younger than her new husband. Even though their wedding had taken place in New York state, close to West Point, Allan had neither invited Edgar to the ceremony nor bothered to visit him.

Now that Fanny was dead and Poe was out on his own, Allan was ready to move forward. He had become involved with a woman named Elizabeth Wills after Fanny's death and before his second marriage. He had two children, twins, with Elizabeth. Louise was unconcerned about these illegitimate children, and she and Allan looked forward to having a family of their own. Unlike Edgar, Elizabeth's twins and any children Allan would have with Louise would be his blood relatives. Allan figured this was the perfect time to rid himself of the financial and emotional drain of Edgar. He wrote to Edgar that he was through with him for good.

Edgar wrote back immediately, pleading with Allan not to give up on their relationship. He insinuated that the only reason he had written the letter implying Allan was a drunk was because his feelings were hurt: "The time in which I wrote it was within a half hour after you had embittered every feeling of my heart against you by your abuse of my *family,* and myself, under your own roof—and at a time when you knew that my heart was almost breaking."

Poe felt victimized—he believed Allan had not given him the attention or the opportunities he should have. He also felt hurt and abandoned. Faced with the possibility of being cut off from John Allan forever, Poe acted—perhaps rashly—to try to get Allan's attention again.

Up until this point, Poe's career at West Point had been exemplary. He had excellent grades and good relationships with his peers and the faculty. But, in a desperate bid to keep John Allan in his life, he informed his old guardian that he wanted to resign from West Point. Just as he needed Allan's permission to leave the Army before, he needed Allan's permission to leave West Point. He warned Allan that if he denied him permission he would simply walk out. "From the time of this writing," he told Allan, "I shall neglect my studies and duties."

Poe began a deliberate campaign to do just that, chalking up as many bad conduct marks as it was possible to attain. He had imagined that a brilliant career at West Point might finally give John Allan reason to be proud of and love him, but any hope of that happening seemed futile. To make matters worse, John Allan ignored his letters and pleas.

Poe quickly piled up so many offenses that he was brought before a general court-martial in January 1831. Accused of gross neglect of duty, absence from academic duties, and disobedience of orders, he was found guilty of all charges and expelled.

During his final days at West Point, Poe had written many amusing sketches of his teachers. He convinced half of the cadets at the academy to give him a dollar and a quarter each to pay for the printing of a volume of his latest poems. Many of the cadets thought they were paying to have a collection of those humorous sketches printed and wanted their money back when they found out the truth—even though the book was dedicated "To the U.S. Corps of Cadets." As usual, Edgar did not have any money to give them. He was saved by the kindly superintendent, who allowed him to stay on at West Point until the end of February in order to earn enough money to cover his latest debts. (Cadets received a weekly stipend.)

The new volume of poetry was entitled *Poems by Edgar A. Poe* and was nearly twice as long as *Al Aaraaf.* The book was labeled a second edition because it had revised versions of both "Tamerlane" and "Al Aaraaf." The few reviewers who commented on it pronounced it even more odd and obscure than his last collection.

When the time came for Poe to leave West Point for good, he had nowhere to go. He went to New York for a short while, and then back to Baltimore. He appealed once more to John Allan for funds, reminding him that if he had only given permission for him to leave the academy, Poe would have received thirty dollars in traveling expenses. Now, as usual, he was broke and bereft. John Allan did not reply.

Edgar Poe had lost two families: the Allan family, which would go on without him, and the family at West Point, which would also thrive in his absence. Perhaps it would be possible to find the family he so craved in Baltimore, the city of his father's ancestors.

Chapter Four

"Muddy" and Virginia

In 1831, Baltimore was a small but thriving city with a bustling harbor, clean, attractive streets, and handsome brick houses. It was also home to an important railway, the Baltimore and Ohio Railroad, which employed what was then a novelty: a steam-powered locomotive. Impressively, Baltimore's Catholic Church owned the largest organ in the country. More importantly to Poe, Baltimore was the home of sympathetic relatives, including his seventy-five-year-old grandmother—the widow of General David Poe—and her forty-one-year-old daughter Maria Clemm, Edgar's aunt.

A widow herself, Maria took care of her mother, who was an invalid, and the two children who were still at home: Edgar's first cousins Henry, who was thirteen, and Virginia, who was nine. Maria made money any honest way she could, mostly by sewing and dressmaking. Because she had been married to General Poe, Edgar's grandmother received a military pension that was just enough to keep the family from slipping into poverty.

Poe thought highly of Aunt Maria, and came to affectionately call her "Muddy." Maria's own mother had recently died and Poe admired the way Maria coped: "attending her [mother] during her long and tedious illness with a Christian and martyr-like fortitude," he wrote a cousin, "and with a constancy of attention, and unremitting affection, which must exalt her character in the eyes of all who know her."

This was the family that Edgar appealed to for help. He had nowhere else to go. Maria and her family occupied the top floor of a small, neat house on Wilks Street in a part of town called Mechanics Row (now Little Italy). Apparently there was room for Edgar. Maria, taking pity on him, allowed him to stay, and Edgar offered to do what he could to increase the family's coffers in return. Surely a large part of his decision to relocate to Baltimore was that it offered him the opportunity to spend time with his brother, William Henry Poe.

Henry had been raised in Baltimore but had gone to sea when he was a teenager, actually having the adventures that Edgar could only pretend he had. Like Edgar, Henry was interested in poetry and literature and had many friends among the literary set in Baltimore. He was also a writer, and several of his poems and short stories had been published in local journals. Some of Henry's poems are startlingly similar to Edgar's, even down to the exact wording of certain phrases and even whole paragraphs. Possibly, these were the results of a collaboration between the two brothers, or Edgar may have allowed Henry to publish some of Edgar's verses under his own name.

Edgar had appealed to Henry for help a few times over the past years, but the latter was never in any condition to assist him. Henry had begun drinking alcohol heavily in his early twenties. Now reunited with the brother that he felt

Poe's beloved aunt, Maria Clemm. *(Ingram-Poe Collection, University of Virginia Library.)*

so close to, Edgar could only watch as Henry drank himself to death. By August of 1831, William Henry Poe was dead from cirrhosis of the liver at the age of twenty-four. To Edgar this loss was one more crushing blow.

Edgar had trouble finding work in Baltimore, although he pursued teaching and editorial positions. Desperate for cash, he not only wrote to John Allan begging for funds, but had his Aunt Maria do the same on his behalf. "I am perishing—absolutely perishing for want of aid," Edgar wrote Allan. "And yet I am not idle—nor addicted to any vice—nor have I committed any offense against society which would render me deserving of so hard a fate. For God's sake pity me, and save me from destruction." Once again, John Allan refused.

Three years had passed since their last meeting when Edgar learned that his former guardian was ill. By this time Allan and his second wife had three small children. Legend has it that Poe rushed to Moldavia and tried to see Allan, who was then fifty-four, but was rebuffed by the new Mrs. Allan. Edgar brushed past her and entered Allan's bedroom, only to have the older man order him out of the house. A week later, Allan died.

A special commission had to be formed to determine the exact worth and details of Allan's complicated estate, which was finally estimated at around seven hundred fifty thousand dollars. Allan's legitimate children inherited the bulk of that money. Louise received Moldavia and interests in other estates and plantations, some land, several hundred slaves, bank stock, and a gold mine waiting to be worked. There were bequests to other relatives in the U.S. and abroad. Edgar received nothing.

Poe had always assumed that some day he, too, would have wealth and power, an end at last to his miserable poverty, but it was not to be. He never got over his disappointment and bitterness, though he tried to put a brave face on it. He described the situation this way: "Brought up to no profession, and educated in the expectation of an immense fortune (Mr. A. having been worth $750,000) the blow has been a heavy one, and I had nearly succumbed to its influence, and yielded to despair. But by the exertion of much resolution I am now beginning to look upon the matter in a less serious light, and although struggling still with many embarrassments, am enabled to keep up my spirits."

One bright spot was his first short story publication in 1836. Poe had submitted "Metzengerstein" to a short story contest sponsored by the *Saturday Courier.* While the story did not win the contest, the editors liked it enough to publish it. "Metzengerstein" is a largely autobiographical story of a young orphaned baron who burns down the stables of an elderly count, who the boy hates and envies because of his wealth. The count is killed in the blaze, but his spirit returns in the form of a demonic horse. The reader does not need to work very hard to assume the young baron is Edgar and the count, John Allan.

Poe submitted several of the stories from a collection called "The Tales of the Folio Club" to a contest sponsored by the Baltimore *Saturday Visitor.* The winning entry was Poe's "MS. Found in a Bottle." Another story from the same collection, "The Visionary" (also known as "The Assignation"), marked Poe's first appearance in a national magazine, *Lady's Book.* These early stories all show hallmarks of the style Poe would make famous. They are haunted by ghosts, touched by the supernatural, and feature various characters escaping—or failing to escape—the gruesome clutches of death.

It was fortunate for Poe that the magazine industry in America was at the beginning of an explosive period of growth. Within a few years, readers could choose from thousands of periodicals of all kinds. The public was better educated and better read than before, which created a strong demand for reading material. The spreading of railroads across the country made it easier for magazines to be distributed. But perhaps most importantly, there was no such thing as copyright law. This meant anyone could publish a version of someone else's work for only the cost of the printing. Verses were routinely attributed to authors not their own, and entire books were published as supplements to magazines—printed on cheap paper and circulated widely thanks to low postage rates. The written word was everywhere.

Poe hoped to cash in on this boom as best he could. One of the first periodicals he contacted was the *Southern Literary Messenger,* which had been founded by a Richmond printer named Thomas Willis White. White needed help with the editorial aspects of the magazine, but was afraid an experienced editor would seize power away from him. White liked Poe's suggestions, however, and after publishing some of his short pieces, added the young man to his staff at a salary of sixty dollars a month. Poe relocated to Richmond, hoping to send for his cousin Virginia and his aunt Maria at the earliest opportunity.

By this time Poe had not only become convinced that his thirteen-year-old cousin Virginia was his soul mate, he wanted her to be his wife. He was a desperately lonely young man who felt a marriage would cement his relationship to his cousin and aunt. He had lost his parents, his foster parents, and his brother. He was looking for a family he could make his own forever.

Poe had become so close to his Aunt Maria, his "Muddy," that she thought of him as her own son. Later he would refer to her, and introduce her to people, as his mother. While Poe began working at the *Southern Literary Messenger,* Maria was still in Baltimore, struggling with poverty. Though she cared deeply for Edgar, she worried he would not be able to support all three of them if they joined him in Richmond.

The Poes had another cousin, Neilson Poe, who was a newspaper editor. He suggested to Maria that she and Virginia stay in Maryland and come to live with him and his family. Virginia could receive a proper education there and Neilson could offer them stability and security.

Maria wrote to Edgar suggesting that it would be for the best if she and Virginia accepted Neilson's offer. Edgar became hysterical after he read Maria's letter. He saw his family eroding in front of his eyes. He wrote Maria that he could not bear the thought of never seeing Virginia again, which he felt certain would happen if she moved in with Neilson. He was convinced that Neilson was jealous of him and wanted to destroy him. "Are you sure Virginia would be more happy?" he wrote Maria. "Do you think anyone could love her more dearly than I? She will have far—very far better opportunities of entering into society here than with [Neilson Poe]. Everyone here receives me with open arms."

Poe went on to say that he had already made arrangements for them both to come to Richmond, and had secured a little house in which the three of them could live together. He promised that his new position at the *Messenger* would give him enough money to take care of them. If that was not enough, he said that he would certainly commit suicide if he had to be alone in the world once again. "What have I *to live for?*" he asked Maria, "Among strangers with *not one soul to love me.*"

Despondent, Poe began neglecting his duties at the *Messenger* and drinking copious amounts of alcohol in the evenings. When he could no longer stand being separated from Virginia and Maria, he went back to Baltimore in late September to persuade the women to return to Richmond with him. He was in Baltimore for less than a month, during which time he and Virginia took out a marriage license. There is no record indicating they actually married then, but when Poe went back to Richmond, he had both Maria and Virginia in tow.

On May 16, 1836, Poe and Virginia were married— possibly for the second time. She was fourteen, though their marriage certificate shows her to be twenty-one. He was twenty-seven. In the beginning of the nineteenth century, it was not uncommon for young women to marry older men, though fourteen was probably at the very low end of the scale. Nor was it unusual or considered improper for first cousins to wed. However, Poe's relationship with Virginia, like his relationships with most of the women in his life, seems to have been more spiritual than sexual in nature. He needed her to satisfy his emotional needs and to help create the sense of security and stability he craved. Poe later intimated that his marriage to Virginia was never consummated.

Now responsible for a family, Poe returned to the *Messenger* to beg for his old job back. His sudden departure had caused serious production problems for the

This photo of Main Street in Richmond, Virginia shows the city as it looked around the time Poe lived there. *(The Cook Collection.)*

publication, but White saw Poe as a surrogate for his own son who had died at nineteen from cholera. White liked Poe and was willing to hire him back on the condition that he never get drunk again. Poe agreed.

Whether the house Poe earlier claimed to have secured had been rented to someone else during his absence, or whether Poe had been exaggerating the situation, Virginia, Maria, and a newly sober Poe lived more or less happily in rooms in a boarding house that cost nine dollars a week. The only thing that bothered Poe was that he had little time to work on his own manuscripts. He had written a few stories in the months before coming to work at the *Messenger.* Some of these he published in the magazine.

In the early 1830s, the United States was on the verge of what came to be known as the American Renaissance. Poet and essayist Ralph Waldo Emerson gave a speech at Harvard in 1837 that signaled the birth of a uniquely American literary and philosophical mindset. Emerson called on artists, writers, and philosophers to break free of the rigid traditions of European thought and to inaugurate an American ideal—a way of thinking that would both reflect and create the intellectual culture of this new country, and that would be in keeping with the wide open spaces and rich possibilities of its land. Emerson was one of the founders of what became known as the Transcendentalist movement. Its followers believed that there was divinity in all things, and that what mattered was not material objects themselves but the way certain objects could help people become aware of transcendent beauty, goodness, and truth.

Poe initially scoffed at the Transcendentalists. Their philosophy contained a fundamental optimism that Poe did not share. Rather, he focused on writing many different kinds of pieces, believing that readers desired a variety of entertaining tales. Poe's writing was closely aligned with his desire to make money and to reach the widest possible audience.

The early stories Poe published in the *Messenger* included both the grotesque and the fanciful, and provided a sharp contrast to the staid and sentimental pieces to which readers were accustomed. "Berenice" (1835) is a gloomy story about a man who becomes obsessed with his cousin, whom he feels he must marry. He is also obsessed with her teeth. When the woman is accidentally buried alive, the man cannot resist his overwhelming compulsion to dig up her grave and, using pliers, extract all of her teeth. The story "Morella" (1835) tells of a woman who is eerily reborn as her own baby.

"The Unparalleled Adventure of One Hans Pfaall" (1835) is more lighthearted—it centers on a dwarf who is so desperate to flee his persistent creditors that he flies to the moon in a balloon. It seems likely that Poe's inspiration for the story came from his own experiences as a debtor. Notably, this story has often been pointed to as the beginning of modern science fiction because it is filled with technical details (many of which Poe copied directly from treatises in technical journals). While Jules Verne is often acknowledged as the first writer of science fiction, his works were published later and clearly show Poe's influence.

But it was not his stories that earned Poe a reputation in the *Messenger*. Embittered over how John Allan and fate had treated him, and anxious to make a name for himself, Poe used his position as editor to become one of the bluntest and most insightful literary critics in America.

Chapter Five

Hatchet Man

As the chief reviewer at the *Southern Literary Messenger,* Poe was absolutely fearless. He would criticize any work deserving of it, regardless of how powerful the writer or publisher was. Because he had few friends, he worried less about making enemies than most ambitious editors and critics. Poe knew he was a fine judge of literary worth and believed it his duty to speak the truth about what he read. Reviews were one of the few ways people had to learn about new books. He saw himself as a kind of gatekeeper with an obligation to keep poorly written and worthless books from surviving. He was also intent on making sure his own writing was widely read. The best way to increase subscriptions to the magazine was to speak not just the truth, but sensational truth.

Poe seemed to take a particularly savage delight in tearing apart the most highly touted new works, the ones other critics had given the best reviews. He described one such book as being "too purely imbecile to merit an extended critique." Though his own publications were just as likely to be riddled with mistakes, he was always quick to point out the grammatical errors in someone else's work—and to explain how they should be fixed. Part of this was his righteous indignation over unworthy books getting attention and making their authors rich. Part of it was simple jealousy.

Poe set himself against the way the literary world worked, in which a few powerful (and generally wealthy) editors, publishers, and writers were able to make the authors they preferred famous by using their positions to praise the authors' works. Success in the literary world could sometimes depend as much upon connections as upon talent. Poe was ruthless in attacking books and poetry written by members of this network—unless the author was someone who could help his own career. As much as Poe deplored nepotism and favoritism, he was very interested in using his few friends and connections to his own advantage. He ranted about editors who used their publications to champion their own writings, but Poe would write favorable reviews about his own work and have those published under pseudonyms.

The literary world and much of the reading public were sharply divided in their opinion of Poe as a critic. Many people admired his frankness and saw him as scrupulously honest and forthright. To these admirers, Poe was incorruptible by outside influences and never influenced by power, prestige, or prevailing opinion. Poe's detractors, however, saw him as a tireless egoist, interested mostly in promoting himself. To them, he was anxious for publicity and attention no matter what he had to do to get it. Even the publisher of the *Messenger* later claimed that Poe rarely read any book all the way through to the end, basing his reviews instead on his own impressions and what he thought would most engage his readers. Poe used his position as a critic to make a name for himself. For better or worse, most literate people in America soon knew who he was.

One of the regrets that haunted Poe was knowing that he could have been a rich and powerful man if only he had inherited what he thought was rightfully his—John Allan's estate. He would have been able to use his own wealth and connections to put himself forward as others did. In Poe's mind, this unfair twist of fate meant he was entitled to do virtually anything to get ahead. This included using the very methods he found so odious when employed by others.

One of the main accusations Poe used against other writers—particularly those enjoying fame and fortune—was that they were plagiarists. Here Poe's own hypocrisy is revealed. He would on occasion lift whole paragraphs from encyclopedias or journals and insert them into his work. Generally these were dry, academic and technical reports which he should have simply quoted from instead of copying. In his defense, many of the pieces he stole from were not attributed to any particular author. Poe may have felt this made it a lesser form of plagiarism, if, indeed, any.

Poe generally plagiarised only from works of nonfiction. However, on at least one occasion he took material from another writer's novel and placed it into one of his own stories. The last paragraph of Poe's "Premature Burial" is, except for a few minor changes, taken from a passage in the book *Stanley,* by the author Horace Binney Wallace, writing under the pseudonym William Landor. Poe often lifted odd items from Landor's writings for the marginalia he contributed to various magazines. These short passages were used to fill up what would otherwise be empty space on the page. When Poe ran out of his own ideas, he would simply use something of Landor's that had been published years before.

Though recognizing Poe's plagiarism is a clue to understanding the insecurity hiding behind his bravado, the vast majority of his published work, fiction and nonfiction, was completely original. Much of Poe's genius lay in his ability to transform traditional character types into mesmerizing and unique psychological profiles.

Poe wrote his fiction and poetry in the gothic tradition, which had been popular for nearly fifty years before he took it up. Gothic novels were embraced in America, Britain, and Germany—Mary Wollstonecraft Shelley's *Frankenstein,* published earlier in the century, and Bram Stoker's *Dracula,* published near its end, are two famous examples. In America, the leading writer of gothic tales before Poe was Charles Brockden Brown, who wrote the novel *Edgar Huntley.*

Gothic writing is typified by certain conventions, including a fascination with psychology, settings that reflect the mental states of the characters, ghostly visions, and haunting of the living by the dead. Some of

Poe's stories were variations of the popular sensational tales that featured people caught helplessly in horrifying predicaments—being buried alive, for example. But Poe always put his own stamp on these conventions and expanded upon them with uncommon intelligence and brash ingenuity. His genius is evident in the wonderful way he employed language, rhythm, and tone in so many of his stories. He was one of the first writers to use language as attentively and effectively in his stories as he did in his poetry. Furthermore, Poe's ability to create rich atmospheres and vivid, unusual characters distinguished him from the gothic writers who had come before.

Unfortunately for Poe, money did not accompany his growing fame. He remained on the edge of a financial precipice for most of his life. He was never paid very much for his stories, and though he made the *Messenger* a success, he did not reap much fiscal reward from it. Poe found it difficult to support both Maria and Virginia— especially since his young wife was often ill. He fell back into his old habit of borrowing money from family and friends, many of whom were never repaid.

During the eighteen-month period Poe worked for the *Messenger* he had an enormous impact on the publication. He brought to it a much-needed creative, innovative spirit. He invited prominent writers to contribute work and made sure the publication had the right look and few grammatical errors. And it was Poe who wrote the reviews that had brought so many curious readers to the *Messenger* in the first place. Soon it had a large circulation—over five thousand subscriptions—and was considered one of the more important and prestigious literary journals in the country. Thomas Willis White acknowledged Poe's contributions by officially making him the editor.

White's initial excitement about Poe's work soon began to fade, however. Despite the paid subscriptions for the *Messenger,* White's debts continued to mount. White's wife developed cancer of the uterus, which put a strain not only on his emotions but also on his finances. The outrage Poe's reviews generated made White worry about libel suits. Finally, it became obvious that Poe had begun drinking again.

Poe gave his version of events in a letter to the physician and editor Dr. J. E. Snodgrass: "while I resided in Richmond, and edited the *Messenger,* I certainly did give way, at long intervals, to the temptation held out on all sides by the spirit of Southern conviviality. My sensitive temperament could not stand an excitement which was an everyday matter to my

Thomas Willis White, owner of the *Southern Literary Messenger. (Harry Ransom Research Center, University of Texas, Austin.)*

companions. In short, it sometimes happened that I was completely intoxicated. For some days after each excess I was invariably confined to bed."

Much has been made of Poe's fondness for alcohol. He might have suffered from a high sensitivity to alcohol that caused him to become easily intoxicated, after only one or two drinks. He might have been unable to stop drinking once he started, which is a symptom of alcoholism. It is clear that he tried to resist the temptation to drink at different times in his life, which is also characteristic of alcoholics. When he failed to stay sober, he usually blamed his friends and acquaintances for coaxing him back into it. He had a history of improper behavior while drunk—making public scenes, hurling accusations at the women he loved, and often spending several days afterwards in bed, unable to work.

Though Poe had promised White he would stay sober, he was unable to keep that promise. Richmond held a lot of unpleasant memories for him. The offices of the *Messenger* were just down the block from what had once been the House of Ellis and Allan. John Allan's new family still lived in luxury nearby in Moldavia, off of wealth Poe thought should have been his. There were many in Richmond who remembered his earlier days as a debtor. It was harder in Richmond than anywhere else for Poe to forget the insults and slights—both real and imagined—that he had endured.

When White fired him from the *Messenger,* it may have come as a relief to Poe. He thought there were better opportunities elsewhere. Although his brief term at the

University of Virginia and few months at West Point hardly added up to a first-class education, he knew that he had a first-class mind. He educated himself by reading books, journals, and encyclopedias, and thought himself at least the intellectual equal of most people and superior to many. Most of his readers thought he was every bit the scholar and intellectual his writings suggested he was. To such a thinker, the *Messenger* should be no more than a stepping stone.

With a view toward furthering his career, Poe moved his family to Greenwich Village in New York City. Even in 1837, Greenwich Village was the bohemian section of the city where many artists of different types took up residence. There, Poe worked on what would be his first and only novel, *The Narrative of Arthur Gordon Pym of Nantucket.* White serialized the first chapter in the *Messenger* to demonstrate that he bore Poe no ill will.

Poe found it difficult to break into the literary establishment of New York, although he pursued any opportunity relentlessly. It was even harder to find steady employment. An economic depression had forced many of the banks in New York and across the United States to close when so many people tried to withdraw their money that the banks ran out of cash. The bank failures sent even more people into a panic. There were few jobs to be had during this depression, even fewer in the world of publishing. The New York publishing house of Harper and Brothers had decided to publish *The Narrative of Arthur Gordon Pym of Nantucket,* but then had to postpone doing so because of the depression. Poe placed just two stories during the year he lived in New York—it was a depressing and difficult time.

Poe felt deeply the responsibility he had assumed for Maria and "Sissy," as he called Virginia. He had convinced them to reject Neilson Poe's offer of food and shelter and now he was determined to find a way to provide for them. He was so discouraged by the lack of opportunities in publishing that he decided to seek his fortune in another field entirely. He wrote to James Kirke Paulding, the secretary of the navy, and asked him for help in getting a job. Paulding was a member of literary circles in New York and Poe had presumably become acquainted with him there.

Even as Paulding was mulling over Poe's desperate request, Harper and Brothers at last came out with an edition of *Arthur Gordon Pym.* In the novel, the title character is hidden by a friend named Augustus in the hold of his father's boat. What begins as a cramped, uncomfortable situation turns into a desperate one when some of the men revolt and kill off most of the crew. Once discovered, young Pym manages to stay alive by befriending one of the mutineers, Dirk Peters. In order to distract the mutineers while the trio of Pym, Augustus, and Peters prepare to take over the ship, Pym disguises himself as the corpse of one of the sailors.

In the book's most macabre sequence, the sailors come upon a ship only to discover that the men on board, who all seem to be moving and waving, are actually corpses being fed upon by seagulls. The birds' jerking movements make the sailors appear to be alive.

Pym and the others are eventually picked up by a schooner, and wind up on an island whose natives at first seem awed and friendly but later set a trap that leads to most of the sailors being buried alive. Pym and Dirk Peters manage to escape the island and sail towards the North Pole, where they encounter all sorts of strange phenomena.

Two "missing" chapters (the novel is presented as nonfiction) leave the final fate of the two men a mystery. Many years later, Poe's admirer Jules Verne took up the story where Poe left off. In Verne's sequel, Dirk Peters, who has survived, sails back to the Antarctic to find the body of Pym pinned to a magnetic mound by the musket that is slung about his shoulder.

Poe's only novel is not as successful as his greatest short stories; even Poe came to think it did not represent him at his best. The early sections are harrowing and suspenseful, but the middle chapters become somewhat tedious and the final sections are too obscure in their descriptions to cast the kind of shuddery spell over the reader that Poe intended. His descriptive powers are otherwise in fine display throughout most of the book, and it does carry a certain air of mystery and dread.

Much like his short stories, Poe's novel relied upon certain autobiographical details. The main character, Pym, is very similar to Poe himself in background and up-bringing—or at least to Poe's preferred version of these. Poe's mother Eliza had once appeared in a play entitled *Tekeli,* and in Poe's novel the islanders and the seagulls both cry out "Tekeli-li." Although in its day the book did not have the impact Poe might have hoped for—and he made very little money from it—it strongly influenced such later writers as Verne, H. P. Lovecraft, and others.

One of Poe's most famous stories, "Ligeia," was published in a Baltimore magazine, *American Museum,* in September of 1838. Ligeia is the dead wife of the narrator, who tries and finally succeeds in forcing her spiritual essence into the body of his second wife, Rowena, as she lies dying. Whatever the merits of the story, it is chiefly famous because of its containing Poe's superb poem "The Conqueror Worm." In the story, the poem is supposed to have been written by Ligeia shortly before her own death. With vivid imagery and great dramatic intensity, the poem imagines a theater wherein the patrons are treated to a macabre spectacle onstage as the actors are devoured by a giant "blood-red" worm. The end of the poem reveals "That the play is the tragedy 'Man,' / And its hero the conqueror Worm."

The message of the poem seems to be that death (as symbolized by the maggot) conquers everyone in his time, but also that death should not be feared. The poem suggests that death is only the natural, inevitable ending of life, and that life is nothing more than a play put on for the entertainment of the gods.

Chapter Six

Washington Follies

Founded originally by the Quaker leader William Penn, Philadelphia was the first city in the nation to have streets laid out in a grid pattern. By the time Poe moved there in 1838, it also had gas lighting in its streets and houses and was home to the progressive Moyamensing Prison, a large Navy Yard, and several theaters, museums, and music halls.

After his disappointments in New York City, thirty-year-old Poe moved his family to Philadelphia in hopes of finding work. Eventually, they were able to set up a little house of their own on the outskirts of the city near Locust Street. Virginia was sixteen, going on seventeen, and impressed those who met her with the refinement she had gained by Poe's tutoring. She had a beautiful singing voice. She and Maria did their best to keep up their home and live frugally while Edgar fruitlessly looked for work.

Finally, Poe contacted Englishman William Evans

Burton, a part-time actor and the editor of *Burton's Gentleman's Magazine.* The magazine featured articles on sports and the outdoor life as well as a range of poems and stories. Burton saw himself as a rugged, self-made man and had no patience for whiners. He resented the way Poe presented himself as a pitiable, hard-luck case in his letters. Burton had endured his own share of problems in life, he said, and had done so without complaining. Still, Burton knew Poe might be able to bring some polish—and readers—to *Gentleman's Magazine,* and agreed to take him on. He hired Poe as Assistant Editor and put Poe's name next to his own on the masthead. For his part, Poe had to swallow his pride to work for Burton—the only entirely negative review Burton had ever printed (and had most likely written himself) had been of *Arthur Gordon Pym.*

Burton was proud that the *Gentleman's Magazine* had a reputation for writing fair and unbiased reviews and wanted Poe to carry on in that tradition. Nevertheless, Poe continued to write his savage reviews, attacking such respected writers as Henry Wadsworth Longfellow and Washington Irving. Oddly, after he had lambasted their work, Poe often wrote to his victims to ask them to endorse his own latest work. He begged Irving for "*even a word or two* . . . [that] would ensure me that public attention which would carry me on to fortune hereafter, by ensuring me fame at once." Poe also continued make baseless accusations of plagiarism about other writers, all the while copying entire pages from other sources and printing them under his own name.

BURTON'S

GENTLEMAN'S MAGAZINE.

EDITED BY

WILLIAM E. BURTON AND EDGAR A. POE.

VOLUME V.

FROM JULY TO DECEMBER.

By a gentleman, we mean not to draw a line that would be invidious between high and low, rank and subordina-
tion, riches and poverty. No. *The distinction is in the mind.* Whoever is open, just, and true; whoever is of a
humane and affable demeanour; whoever is honorable in himself, and in his judgment of others, and requires no
law but his word to make him fulfil an engagement;—such a man is a gentleman;—and such a man may be found
among the tillers of the earth as well as in the drawing rooms of the high born and the rich.

DE VERE.

PHILADELPHIA.
PUBLISHED BY WILLIAM E. BURTON,
DOCK STREET, OPPOSITE THE EXCHANGE.

1839.

The frontispiece of an issue of *Burton's* with Poe sharing credit on the masthead. *(Fales Library, New York University.)*

One of the features of *Burton's Gentleman's Magazine* that helped make Poe a household name was the cryptogram. Cryptograms are messages written in code. For example, if each letter of the alphabet is replaced by a corresponding number (A=1, B=2, C=3, etc.), the encrypted message 5-4-7-1-18 1-12-12-1-14 16-15-5 can be decoded to read "Edgar Allan Poe." Poe greatly enjoyed these devices and included some in every issue. He challenged readers to make up their own and submit them for him to solve, boasting that he could not be beat. Most of the cryptograms he received were fairly elementary, which was lucky for him. The authors used simple substitutions or encoded common phrases that were easy to recognize. Though Poe did have a flair for cryptograms, he was not the expert solver he claimed to be.

Poe also wrote some of his most famous and original works during this period. Poe's editorial duties for Burton left him plenty of time to devote to his own work. Although his salary was not large, it was enough to keep him and his family comfortable. He made a little extra money writing reviews and miscellaneous pieces, and the family of three finally enjoyed some measure of security. Poe's creative juices flowed as they never had before, producing such fiction as "The Fall of the House of Usher" (1839), "William Wilson" (1839), and "The Murders in the Rue Morgue" (1841).

"The Fall of the House of Usher" is one of Poe's most morbid and compelling stories. The neurotic Roderick Usher summons a boyhood friend (the narrator) to his home where he tells the friend that his own twin sister,

Madeline Usher, is about to die. The atmosphere of the story is alive with gothic conventions. The Ushers live in a gloomy, enormous mansion, full of mysterious noises and chilly drafts. When Madeline succumbs to her illness, Usher and the narrator put her body in a crypt below the house. Over the next week the narrator notes that Roderick is behaving very strangely. Late

William Evans Burton employed Poe as Assistant Editor of *Burton's Magazine. (The New York Historical Society, New York City.)*

one stormy night, he realizes it is because Madeline has been interred prematurely, in other words, buried alive. Usher, whose hearing is abnormally acute, has been driven to madness by the frantic, desperate scratching of his sister in her coffin.

That same stormy night, Madeline breaks free of her coffin. She makes her way upstairs, attacks her brother, and they both fall to the floor, dead. The narrator flees the cursed house of Usher, as a fissure in the wall widens and the entire structure collapses to be swallowed up by a gloomy pond.

"The Fall of the House of Usher" uses the technique of doubling, which is another common gothic convention.

For instance, Roderick and Madeline are twins, mirrors are constantly referenced in the story, and when the narrator first sees the house he also sees its reflection in the pond. This technique reminds the reader that the past is never gone—the things we have done always haunt us.

The inspiration for Poe's fascinating and suspenseful story "William Wilson" was a short article by Washington Irving that Poe expanded upon. Poe's hero is haunted by the materialization of his own conscience, which follows him about throughout his life and appears at highly dramatic—and unfortunate—moments. The story is full of autobiographical details, especially from Poe's school days. "William Wilson," like "House of Usher," uses the technique of doubling to comment on the question of identity. The title character believes another person shares his name, only to eventually find that other person is in fact himself. Poe's own life was a kind of doubling—on one hand, he was a distinguished man of letters. On the other, he could be a drunken, embarrassing boor and a nasty, envious critic.

Poe worked for Burton for a year before the two men quarreled and Poe left. Burton had considered selling the magazine in order to concentrate on his acting career, but he did not tell Poe about his plans. By the same token, Poe planned to start his own publication, without informing Burton. When each discovered the other's subterfuge, he was furious. A bitter dispute was resolved when Poe either quit or was fired.

During his tenure with Burton, Poe finally managed to get a collection of his stories published under the title

Tales of the Grotesque and Arabesque (1839). For payment he received only twenty free copies of the book—the publishing house would keep any profit—but the collection of stories garnered many excellent reviews and was compared favorably to Nathaniel Hawthorne's macabre 1837 collection *Twice-Told Tales*. The notices for the book reaffirmed Poe's conviction that he was wasting his time writing for *Burton's Gentleman's Magazine,* which he had always considered vulgar and lowbrow. Poe had also never forgotten Burton's unfavorable review of his novel.

After leaving Burton, Poe began soliciting subscribers and writers for a new magazine he planned to call *Penn.* Though Poe made grand plans for the publication and raised a good amount of money to finance it, the magazine never appeared. Poe was sidelined by an illness, and then another bank failure put an end to his plans. It was time to go looking for work, again.

This time, Poe did not have far to go. Burton had sold his magazine to a young Philadelphia publisher named George Rex Graham. Graham was not yet thirty, but he was both ambitious and smart. He was also generous, and willing to pay the highest salaries in the business to retain the best writers. He offered Poe a job editing *Graham's Lady's and Gentleman's Magazine*—popularly known as *Graham's.*

Graham was a hands-on editor, and wanted Poe only to proofread and write a few reviews. Graham did not tell Poe to reduce the severity of his criticisms, as he knew the public relished each nasty word. Plus, he could see

George Rex Graham, another of Poe's many employers. *(The picture department of the Free Library of Philadelphia.)*

that Poe would temper his barbs with praise when it was earned. As Graham expected, Poe's reviews were popular, and several of them still stand as seminal works in the field of literary criticism. Poe was in many ways single-handedly responsible for transforming literary criticism into the specific and thoughtful genre it is today. Despite his success, it rankled Poe that he was much better known as a critic than as a poet or short story writer.

Today, of course, it is his poetry and short stories that are most remembered. One of the most important stories of his career is "The Murders in the Rue Morgue" (1841), which was first published in *Graham's*. It is considered the first detective story ever written—before it was published, the word "detective" was not used in the English language. Police work was still in its infancy, and many rural areas did not have any kind of law enforcement. The idea of a professional police force, which began in London, was barely ten years old.

Crime fascinated people, especially brutal crime. This fascination was in keeping with the gothic tradition, which was filled with graphic descriptions of murder and death. The newspapers and magazines of Poe's day were quick to include lurid accounts of real-life murders and trials in their pages. Poe combined the popularity of true-crime stories with his own fascination with reason and logic, as evidenced by his obsession with cryptography. He believed that if something was studied carefully enough, even the messiest scene could be understood.

Poe created a detective, C. Auguste Dupin, who was in many ways an idealized version of Poe himself. Dupin appeared in three stories: "The Murders in the Rue Morgue," "The Mystery of Marie Roget" (1843), and "The Purloined Letter" (1845).

In "The Murders in the Rue Morgue," Dupin investigates the ghastly murders of a mother and daughter in Paris. The older woman has been beheaded and the younger woman's body stuffed up a chimney—and the twist is that the crimes were committed in a room locked from the inside. There was no way the killer could have escaped, but no killer remained. Not only was this the first "locked room" mystery but it set the pattern for many mystery stories to come. The hero is an amateur detective and not a police officer; the tale is narrated in the first person by the detective's friend; the detective observes clues that are noticeable to no one else and keeps them to himself until revealing the startling conclusion; and so on. Dupin is a cold, one-dimensional character whose feats of deduction fascinate the reader.

"The Mystery of Marie Roget" was Poe's attempt to use Dupin to solve the real-life murder of a woman named Mary Rogers in New York. Though the story was fictionalized and set in Dupin's Paris, Poe was intent on showing that the most popular theories about the death of Mary Rogers were incorrect. He came up with a new solution, but was unable to actually name the killer. Years later his theory was disproved and he revised the story. Poe's Dupin was one of the first forensic observers, concentrating on the physical evidence of the crime to lead him to the killer.

"The Purloined Letter" has Dupin called to help find an incriminating missive. This story moves the detective genre forward again as Dupin has to learn to be suspicious of even the least likely suspect, to realize that behind one crime can be multiple motives, and to look for clues concealed in plain sight. At the end of this story, the stolen letter is found to have been on the table in front of everyone the entire time—it had just been moved to a different envelope.

During Poe's tenure at *Graham's,* circulation swelled nearly tenfold. Despite this, Poe grew as dissatisfied with his work as he had been when the magazine was under Burton's control. Fearing libel suits or offending advertisers, Graham began asking Poe to tone down his reviews and to praise authors Poe found unworthy. Poe was insulted, and began to grumble that Graham was not paying him enough. Though Graham's salaries were the highest of the era for the work, Poe still found grounds to complain. As he had with *Burton's,* Poe felt this magazine was beneath him. Finally, Poe quit.

Around this time, Poe's wife Virginia was singing for friends one night when she suddenly stopped, coughed, and began to bleed from her mouth. The friends thought she must have ruptured a blood vessel in her throat, which was preferable to the truth—the blood was coming from her lungs. Poe's beloved "Sissy," age nineteen, had tuberculosis.

During the 1840s, tuberculosis, sometimes called the "white plague," accounted for twenty-five percent of all deaths. A disease of the lungs that spread through repeated close contact with someone already infected, tuberculosis ran rampant in cramped and over-crowded cities. Today, medication can usually cure the disease, but then it was almost always a death sentence.

After her first episode, Virginia was bedridden for several weeks. She eventually made a temporary recovery but remained frail and would have frequent relapses, suffering from night sweats, extreme fatigue, and severe coughing spells.

Virginia's illness was extremely difficult for Poe. He became paranoid about her health, alternately refusing to admit she might be sick and then hovering over her, cringing at each cough. "Sissy" was tremendously important to Poe. Though he wooed other women throughout their marriage, he was devoted to her and believed it was her constant attention and charm that kept him sane. He needed his little family of Virginia and Maria. After a job rejection, Poe had once written to his wife: "In my last great disappointment I should have lost my courage *but for you*—my little darling wife you are my *greatest* and *only* stimulus now, to battle with this uncongenial, unsatisfactory and ungrateful life."

Each time Virginia had a relapse, Poe suffered as much emotionally as she did physically. Each recovery brought renewed hope; each inevitable collapse, more dread and fear about the future. Poe suffered such anxiety over his wife's condition and his own financial problems that he was soon drinking more heavily than ever. He had a whole circle of friends—young journalists, actors, and poets—who helped him lose himself in the bottle.

Poe's drinking worried Virginia and Maria. He became restless and irritable, and often disappeared for one or more days. In June of 1842, he went to New York to try to drum up interest in a new collection of his stories. While there, he became inebriated at one of the city's many taverns. He then decided to go visit an old girlfriend in Jersey City, but became disoriented and simply rode back and forth on the ferryboat for hours. He was finally found wandering the woods not too far from the woman's house.

Things continued to spiral downwards. Poe was soon so broke that he could not even afford the fee required to file for bankruptcy. And yet, despite his personal problems, he kept writing.

The influence of Virginia's illness is clear in two

stories from this period. "The Oval Portrait" (originally published in *Graham's* as "Life in Death" in 1842) describes an artist so consumed by painting a life-like portrait of his beloved that he does not notice she is wasting away in front of his eyes. When at last the painting is done, the artist realizes that his model, his inspiration, is dead. Whether Poe felt in some way responsible for Virginia's illness or not, the story is a haunting presage of her death. Though he wanted to provide for his wife and her mother, Poe's true obsession was his desire to establish himself in the literary firmament. Readers have since seen this story as evidence Poe believed his relentless pursuit of fame had killed his wife.

"The Masque of the Red Death" (1842) is one of Poe's undisputed masterpieces. In it, rich, callous revelers entertained by Prince Prospero in his castle discover that even they are not safe from death and horror as the plague—the "Red Death"—that has been devastating the countryside catches up to them. Embodied as a masked figure made up to look like a bloodied victim of the plague, the Red Death itself sweeps through the celebration and finally confronts the evil Prince and his quivering consorts. As dramatic as it is creepy, this fascinating, poetic tale of horror displays Poe's genius for mood and imagery at its best.

"The Masque of the Red Death" is similar to Poe's poem "The Conqueror Worm" in that it portrays death as something inevitable—something that comes for all people, no matter who they are.

In still another effort to find a lasting job, Poe hoped

that some friends could wangle him a job as a clerk in Washington, D. C., in President John Tyler's administration. Besides a guaranteed annual salary, the position would have left him plenty of time to work on his stories. President Tyler's son Robert was a poet himself and an admirer of Poe. Other authors, such as Nathaniel Hawthorne and Herman Melville, had been employed in the United States Custom Service, and Poe wondered if he could secure a similar post. A writer named Frederick W. Thomas, who was a Washington clerk, also greatly admired Poe, and promised to do all he could to help. Despite Poe's best efforts, the job never materialized.

Appearing at the Philadelphia Custom House to speak to the collector of customs, Poe made the mistake of declaring himself to be nonpartisan and apolitical. Perhaps Poe simply did not realize that each administration wanted to fill its ranks with staunch supporters, not people uninterested in politics. It is remarkable that Poe would be unaware of this patronage system, but apparently he was. The names of the new appointees to the Custom House positions were posted in the newspaper. Day after day, Poe waited with increasing impatience to hear from the collector of customs. The man had promised to send a messenger when and if Poe was selected. Finally, Poe realized he had never been asked for his address. Distracted by this disappointment and his wife's health, Poe did no writing, applied for no other jobs, and made no money.

In June of 1843, Poe, tired of waiting, decided to go to Washington, D.C. to appeal to Robert Tyler and perhaps even directly to his father, the president. He also planned to use the occasion to build up interest in the magazine he wanted to publish, which he now planned to call *Stylus.* Borrowing money for the trip, he ran through most of it after only two days in Washington. In his desperation, Poe again turned to alcohol and went on a prolonged drunk, during which he managed to offend and dismay many people who had pledged to help him, including Frederick Thomas and Robert Tyler. Any chance he had of getting a political job was lost.

There were other repercussions from the Washington trip. Poe had managed to interest Thomas C. Clarke in joining him in his *Stylus* venture. Clarke was the successful publisher of the Philadelphia *Saturday Museum Magazine.* He was willing to put up the money for *Stylus* while letting Poe manage the magazine any way he wanted. But when word of the drinking binge in Washington got back to Clarke, he backed down. Poe wrote letters of apology to those he had offended, but the damage had been done. Beneath the jocular tone of these letters, through which Poe tried to save face, there was an almost palpable aura of heartbreak and humiliation.

Broke, mortified, and desperate, Poe was down but not out. As he later wrote Frederick W. Thomas, literature was in his blood. He even tried to couch his failed job hunt as a good thing, which would not induce him to stray from his intended goals:

> Literature is the most noble of professions. In fact, it
> is about the only one fit for a man. For my own part

there is no seducing me from the path. I shall be a *littérateur* at least, all my life; nor would I abandon the hopes which still lead me on for all the gold in California.

Talking of gold and of the temptation at present held out to 'poor devil authors' did it ever strike you that all that is really valuable to a man of letters—to a poet in especial—is absolutely unpurchaseable? Love, fame, the dominion of intellect, the consciousness of power, the thrilling sense of beauty, the free air of Heaven, exercise of body & mind, with the physical and moral health that result—these and such as these are really all that a poet cares for.

Poe's cheerful words masked the reality of his situation: he had no money, few prospects, and the woman he loved was dying.

Chapter Seven

Broadway Journal

Poe was never shy about doing anything posible to promote himself and his work. Upon his return to Philadelphia from his disastrous Washington trip, he set about selling himself to the reading public. He wrote a lengthy autobiographical sketch for the *Saturday Museum* magazine that relayed his life history as he would have liked to have lived it and presented himself to the public in the way he wished to be perceived. According to the sketch, he was a hero and soldier-of-fortune who had many exciting adventures abroad, fought bravely in foreign wars, and was revered as a legend wherever he went.

When the famous thirty-year-old British novelist Charles Dickens came to visit America from London, Poe hounded him for an interview. He hoped to use Dickens to expand his own fame and influence in the United Kingdom. As the meeting between the two giants of literature at Dickens's hotel was going well, Poe boldly asked Dickens if he could help him to find a British publisher for his *Tales of the Grotesque and Arabesque.* Dickens kept his promise to do what he could, but the publishers he tried to interest in Poe's work could not see a profit in a collection of stories by an American author who was unknown in England. In spite of Dickens's well-intentioned efforts, Poe felt betrayed.

When the London *Foreign Quarterly* reviewed Poe's poetry and suggested he merely imitated Tennyson, Poe was further outraged. He was convinced that Dickens himself had written the anonymous review, though he was repeatedly assured this was not the case. Poe was also angry that several of his stories appeared in British publications without his permission and without his being paid. He clung to each of these perceived slights, his paranoia increasing.

In November of 1842, Poe learned that a Harvard graduate named James Russell Lowell planned to publish a new literary magazine in Boston called the *Pioneer*. Lowell, who was only twenty-three, admired Poe's forthrightness as a critic and invited him to send reviews, poems, and fiction for possible publication in the *Pioneer*. He also warned Poe not to make personal, possibly libelous, remarks about the authors in his reviews.

Poe felt a certain admiration for Lowell's poetry and especially for his plans for the *Pioneer*. He began a correspondence with him that reveals his attitude toward his own writing and status as a writer. Poe said that he was "excessively slothful, and wonderfully industrious—by fits. There are epochs when any kind of mental exercise is torture, and when nothing yields me pleasure but solitary communion with the 'mountains and the woods.' ... I have thus rambled and dreamed away whole months, and awake, at last, to a sort of mania for composition. Then I scribble all day and read all night, so long as the disease endures." The *Pioneer* helped Poe become more widely known in New England, but it folded after only three issues.

In addition to several critiques and poems, Lowell published Poe's famous story "The Tell-Tale Heart" (1843). "The Tell-Tale Heart" is a study of a psychotic mind. The narrator is a murderer who has hidden his victim's body under the floorboards of his house. But, as his guilt grows, he imagines he can hear the dead man's heart beating, louder and louder, until he is finally driven to confess his crime to the police. This story has influenced the countless mysteries, films, and comic books that feature a murderer revealing the details of his crime because he is haunted by the deed or the victim.

Another of Poe's masterpieces is "The Pit and the Pendulum" (1843), which he sold to *The Gift,* one of several periodicals based in Philadelphia that Poe wrote for in an effort to stay afloat after leaving *Graham's.* The story describes a man imprisoned in a dungeon during the Spanish Inquisition. He is strapped to a slab and left to die as a heavy, razor-sharp pendulum swings lower and lower over his writhing body. He is saved from being cut in two by the gnawing hordes of hungry rats that nibble at his ropes as well as his flesh. Saved from one gruesome death, he barely has time to take a breath before the walls of his cell begin moving inward, closer

This oil painting of Poe was made around 1845 by Samuel S. Osgood. *(The New York Historical Society, New York City.)*

and closer. At the very last minute, the narrator is saved when the French army rescues him—his death has been averted. The gripping "Pit and the Pendulum" is the ultimate doom-trap story. Horror and thriller writers since have imitated and tried to outdo the terrifying scenario Poe devised for his narrator.

In April 1844, Poe and Virginia left Philadelphia for New York City, where they first stopped at a boarding house on Greenwich Street. Maria had stayed in Philadelphia with Poe's cat Catterina, which was just as well because Poe and his wife had little money. He was determined to make a fresh start in the city that was already becoming known as the publishing and literary capital of the United States. Later, when Poe and Virginia left Manhattan, which they found dirty, and relocated upstate near the Hudson River, they sent for Maria and the cat. For a few months Poe and his loved ones were co-tenants in a house on a two-hundred-acre farm owned by the Brennan family.

From the farmhouse Poe churned out letters and articles, reviews and stories, anything to try to make a living. He was even willing to descend to the "hack" work he felt was beneath him. Poe also tried to insinuate himself into the better-paying and more prestigious markets. He contacted the editor of the New York *Evening Mirror*. Nathaniel Parker Willis was not only a successful essayist and editor, he was also known as the first writer to make a good living from writing professionally for the magazine market. Willis hired Poe as an assistant editor and all-purpose office hand. It was depressing for Poe to write fillers, answer letters, and perform other mundane tasks when he had so much experience in the business, but he was grateful for the salary. On his own time he continued to write stories, including "The Premature Burial" (1844).

As the title implies, the story centers on a man who is terrified of being buried alive— one of Poe's favorite horrors. The character also suffers from catalepsy, a condition characterized by a loss of consciousness accompanied by muscles becoming so stiff that they remain in whatever position they are placed, as happens in the post-death state of rigor mortis. During a bout of catalepsy, the man in Poe's story is indeed mistaken for dead and buried alive.

Nathaniel Willis, editor of the *Evening Mirror*. *(The New York Historical Society.)*

Poe's wife was still very ill at this time, and his fears for her well-being inhabit many of his stories and poems from this period, such as "The Oblong Box" (1844) and "The Raven" (1845). In the latter, one of his best-known poems, the raven that comes to the narrator's window and cries "Nevermore" is a metaphor for endless grief and the eternal memory of a lost loved one. When the narrator asks if someday he will be reunited with the loved one who died, he feels despair at the raven's repeated reply of

"Nevermore." Poe once commented that by pestering the raven for a reply again and again, the narrator is indulging in a kind of sublime self-torture or masochism. The poem also suggests that the dead leave us at peace as long as we remember them, but haunt us whenever we start to forget.

Much of Poe's work concerns death and dying. It was as if Poe was already mourning his wife, aware that her death—and his loneliness—were inevitable.

The publication of "The Raven" was a success. The poem became the talk of New York. All at once Poe, now thirty-six, was almost as famous a poet as he was a critic. Despite the sad story the poem had to tell (and the fact that some critics thought it was a tricky, overrated piece), its cleverness in structure, singsong rhythms, and the general accessibility of its language made it one of the most popular poems ever written. Throughout his life, Poe would be called upon to recite it in his unique style.

Around January of 1845, Poe, Virginia, and Maria moved from the farm back into the city. Over a period of several months they resided variously at 154 Greenwich Street, 195 East Broadway, and 85 Amity Street, not far from Washington Square. Eventually they made their way uptown to Fordham (in what is now known as the Bronx), where they resided in a little cabin that still exists and can be visited today.

The occasion of the move from the farm was Poe's leaving the *Mirror* and going to work for a new weekly publication, the *Broadway Journal*. This magazine was the result of a partnership between editor Charles

Frederick Briggs and publisher John Bisco. The former hired Poe as an assistant editor after both agreed that New York needed a journal that would represent its own writers and interests as opposed to the snobbish literary sects of Boston. Poe told friends that he had a financial interest in the publication, which was not true. He wanted people to think that the *Broadway Journal* was finally his own publication.

Poe put in many hours each day on the *Journal.* He wrote lengthy reviews and even republished some of his own stories, though the policy of the magazine was to avoid reprints. Besides reviewing books and poetry, he now began writing critiques of the theater, too. Undoubtedly he felt that because his parents were actors (although few people knew this fact) he was qualified to sit in judgment of plays. Now that he had his own magazine—or the closest thing to it—his reviews were not only unflinching but positively ferocious. Poe's sour mood was due to a combination of things: Virginia's fluctuating health as well as the fact that his newfound fame from "The Raven" had not increased his coffers by one penny.

While working at the *Mirror,* Poe had begun what would become an almost obsessive, pathological series of attacks on one of America's most beloved and popular poets, Henry Wadsworth Longfellow. At the *Journal* he stepped up the attacks, accusing Longfellow of being not only overrated to the extreme but also guilty of countless plagiarisms. The *Journal*'s editor, Briggs, tried to get Poe to tone down his assaults, but nothing could stop him once he smelled blood. Poe was going to make Longfellow

Poet Henry Wadsworth Longfellow, one of Poe's favorite targets. *(National Park Service, Longfellow National Historical Site.)*

pay for being more successful than he was and for being a graduate of prestigious Harvard. Poe saw Longfellow as the embodiment of what he could have been if he had only had a chance.

Longfellow was the only poet in America who could live comfortably off the income from his books. On top of that he had married an heiress. Longfellow was also an avid abolitionist, in favor of ending the practice of slavery. Like most southerners (and many northerners) in this pre-Civil War period, Poe believed slavery was an important and necessary institution. He added Longfellow's liberal politics to his list of things to attack.

All of literary New York was in an uproar over the articles Poe wrote about Longfellow. Some sided with Longfellow, others with Poe. For his part, Longfellow tried to stay above it all. He realized that Poe wanted a feud for its publicity value. Briggs worried about Longfellow filing a libel suit, but Poe enjoyed all the attention.

Poe quickly became the guest to invite to the fashionable literary salons that were part of upper-class Manhattan society. These salons were run primarily by wealthy women who wished to mingle with writers, artists, and musicians. The artists benefited not only from commissions but also from the free food. Underpaid as ever, Poe would read "The Raven" and then grab as much food as he could.

Several of the women Poe met in these salons were attracted to him. He was short, with an overly large head, but he had piercing gray eyes and dark curly hair. Poe

Fanny Osgood, one of the women Poe befriended in New York. *(The New York Historical Society, New York City.)*

corresponded frequently with several admirers, including two (married) poets, Fanny Osgood and Elizabeth Ellet.

Elizabeth Ellet was jealous of Poe's relationship with Fanny Osgood. When she tried to interfere, Poe insulted her, which made her very angry. She sent her brother to Poe's house to demand that Poe hand over all the letters Ellet had written him. When Poe explained he had already returned the letters, the brother accused him of lying and threatened him with bodily harm. Scared, Poe asked Thomas Dunn English, a poet he knew, to lend him a gun. When he explained why, English laughed at him and called him a liar, saying he doubted Poe had ever had a letter from Elizabeth Ellet. Poe lunged at English and they fought. English beat Poe badly.

The details of the fight were soon fodder for gossip throughout the city. Poe bore the brunt of public censure. He was no longer welcome at parties or salons, and rumors swelled that he was insane. Elizabeth Ellet would remain his enemy for years to come, though Fanny Osgood became a staunch Poe defender.

After being thrown out of the sophisticated literary salons of New York, Poe made arrangements to give a lecture in Boston. Many people saw this as foolishness on his part—Longfellow was one of the mainstays of the Boston literary scene and his friends were all upset about the thrashing Poe had given him. Angry that Poe would presume to enter their territory, they planned a fitting reception for him. By most accounts, Poe's lecture at the Boston Lyceum, a literary society, was a disaster.

Poe had promised to read a new poem, but was unable to write one. He began drinking again, briefly, then pulled himself together for the trip to Boston. There he pretended to have forgotten his manuscript before finally producing one from his trunk, which turned out to be "Al Aaraaf," the poem he had written more than fifteen years earlier. He gave it a new title, but that did not improve the poem. Most of the audience walked out during his reading, until someone kindly suggested he read "The Raven" instead. He did so, and salvaged some of the evening, but the effect was not what he had desired. When he returned to New York, he tried to convince people there he had intended to read the old poem as a way of mocking the Bostonians who hated him.

The *Journal*'s editor, Briggs, was already disenchanted with Poe because of his mean-spirited, nitpicking reviews and his drinking. For these and other reasons Briggs left the *Journal*. The publisher, Bisco, turned to Poe to take his place. Suddenly, Poe really was co-owner and the one and only editor of the *Journal*.

It seemed his dream of owning a publication and running it any way he pleased had come true, but the *Journal* was deeply in debt. Before long, Bisco departed, turning over to Poe all rights and title to the *Journal*. Poe was left on his own to deal with the editorial duties, increasing debts, contributor's demands, submissions, and everything else—without being able to draw a salary. Poe had his own magazine at last—and it was not a dream but a nightmare.

Poe did the best he could, borrowing money from anyone who would give it to him, friends and enemies alike. "I have need of the most active exertion to extricate myself from the embarrassments into which I have already fallen," he wrote one acquaintance. "My object in writing you this note is, (once again) to beg your aid. Of course I need not say that my most urgent trouble is the want of ready money."

Poe filled up the magazine with reprints of his own

reviews, and even ran reviews of books he had not had time to read. Contributors were not paid and circulation dropped drastically. In desperation Poe took on a new partner, Thomas H. Lane, who in return for a half interest agreed to pay off the debts, handle the financial end, and allow Poe autonomy in running the *Journal*.

It was the perfect solution, but Poe ruined it all by going off on a drunken binge that lasted for days and caused him to neglect his duties. Understandably concerned at how his investment would fare, Lane tried to sober Poe up but soon realized it was a hopeless task. Having no other choice but to shut the magazine down, he did so in January of 1846. For the rest of his life, Poe would blame Lane for destroying his dream.

Chapter Eight

"Lord Help My Poor Soul"

In 1845 Wiley and Putnam, a New York publishing house, issued Poe's work under their "Library of American Books" imprint. These inexpensive editions may not have been produced quite as tastefully as Poe might have hoped, but they introduced him to many new readers. The volumes got excellent reviews and even managed to make a little money.

Encouraged by this small success, Poe continued to devote himself to his writing. His story "The Facts in the Case of M. Valdemar" (1845) concerns a mesmerist who puts a dying man under hypnosis and manages to thereby delay the man's death for months. Once out of the trance, the subject literally dissolves—it was only the hypnotism that had been keeping him alive.

Another story, "The System of Doctor Tarr and Professor Fether" (1845), concerns a man who pays a visit to a madhouse to study the doctor there and his radical new approach to mental illness. Noticing how disturbed many

This watercolor portrait of Poe depicts him at the age of thirty-seven. *(Painting by John A. McDouall, Henry E. Huntington Library and Art Gallery.)*

of the staff members seem to be, the visitor finally learns that the inmates are literally running the asylum; the real staff had been imprisoned long ago. Like many of his other stories, this one has engendered countless imitations in the decades since its publication.

The Poe family moved back to the village of Fordham, hoping the peacefulness of the country might be better for Virginia's health. They rented a charming cottage with plenty of green grass and fresh air. Virginia continued to have relapses and then improve, though she never fully regained her strength. Poe, too, was ill during this time—there were even rumors that he was losing his mind. One newspaper printed an item that said Poe had "become deranged" and would soon be committed to a mental institution. It is unclear what actually ailed him, but it seems the combined strain of Virginia's illness and their constant poverty drove him nearly to the breaking point.

Amazingly, one of Poe's most important and rational works came during this difficult time. Probably written in early 1846, "The Philosophy of Composition" was published in *Graham's* in April of that year. It is one of Poe's most important works because it explains concisely and in precise language how he had gone about composing "The Raven." Contrary to Poe's public image as a dissolute, wild, and impulsive person, "The Philosophy of Composition" reveals a serious man with a calculated and deliberate composition process. Poe outlined, line by line, his reasoning for the inclusion of each element of the poem. He stripped away the romantic notion of poetic

An 1884 photograph of the cottage that Poe, Maria, and Virginia rented in Fordham, New York. *(The Bronx County Historical Society.)*

inspiration and said that poetry should be written in a measured, conscious way to achieve the effect desired.

Some of Poe's readers wondered if this essay was a hoax of some kind—they found it hard to reconcile this rational and deliberate writer with the poet they knew. Some Poe fans found "The Philosophy of Composition" disillusioning, stripping away as it did the veil of mystery from his writing process. It was as if he had admitted to composing poetry using mathematical formulas.

Later writers, especially in the French Symbolist school founded by Charles Baudelaire, took Poe's essay as their compositional handbook. From Poe they learned to choose words carefully—not just for their meanings but for their aural impact. The main point Poe made in "The Philosophy of Composition" is his belief that the process of composition should proceed backwards. A writer absolutely had to know what effect she wanted the story or poem to create before writing the first word. He argued that in order for the story or poem to achieve that effect, every single aspect of it had to contribute to the piece's ultimate goal. Every word, every syllable, every sound needed to serve a purpose. Poe was advocating a way of thinking about writing that was analytical and calculating. Good writing, for Poe, was like good carpentry: it came from careful planning, considered choices, and hard work.

To earn some money, Poe began writing for another magazine. *Godey's Lady's Book* was the kind of publication he thought of with contempt, which meant it was extremely popular and full of the kind of writing he thought sentimental and cloyingly sweet. The editors offered him space for a series of articles, which Poe entitled "The Literati of New York City." These were generally very similar to the kinds of reviews he usually wrote, except that he took the genre a step further and included a gossipy, often virulent, description of each person's personality and physical appearance and then offered a few lines of summary about the person's work. Charles Briggs, the man Poe had worked for on the *Broadway Journal,* had his qualifications as an editor described thusly: "Mr. Briggs has never composed in his life three consecutive sentences of grammatical English."

These "Literati" articles were often short, but so scathing as to attract attention. *Godey's* sold out within hours, and Poe was again the talk of the town. Some of his victims, including Briggs, fought back. Briggs published a sketch in the New York *Mirror* in which he described Poe as being barely an inch above five feet tall (when he was really five foot eight) and made fun of his physical appearance: "his tongue shows itself unpleasantly when he speaks earnestly . . . his walk is quick and jerking . . . his hands are singularly small, resembling bird claws."

Poet and editor Thomas Dunn English, with whom Poe had recently engaged in fisticuffs, was so incensed by the things Poe wrote that he too wrote a derisive reply to his sketch in the *Mirror.* English charged that Poe was a drunkard, a plagiarist, and a forger who had been arrested numerous times and had taken money from him under false pretenses.

In return, Poe filed a civil suit for libel against the owners of the *Mirror* in July of 1846. Although much of what English had said about Poe was true, he had, at least, never committed forgery.

Poe made many enemies over the years. Yet he was always able to perceive himself as the victim, never the victimizer. He often worked out his revenge on those he detested in his writing. The narrator of "The Cask of Amontillado" (1846) lures a condescending onetime friend into an ancient vault by promising him a taste of a special wine. Once the man is inside the vault, the narrator uses bricks and mortar to wall up the inebriated man for all time.

"Hop-Frog" (1849) was the last of Poe's masterpieces

and also deals with the theme of revenge. In this story a put-upon dwarf enacts a diabolical revenge against the cruel king and his consorts who mistreat him and his tiny girlfriend, Trippetta. These stories are powerful and gruesome, perhaps all the more so because they so clearly reflect Poe's frustration and anger at his station in life. Though he vented his ire in his infamous "Literati" sketches, Poe seemed to have had a bottomless reservoir of anger toward all those he thought had hurt or cheated him in some way.

In January of 1847, twenty-five-year-old Virginia finally succumbed to her illness. As much as Poe might have tried to prepare himself for it, her long, drawn-out death was excruciating. During this period Poe himself became ill, undoubtedly from his emotional torment over Virginia's hopeless condition.

Virginia was very sick for several months before her death. During that time, Poe was unable to work and the family scraped by on little money. Well-meaning friends took up collections and posted notices of their plight in the newspapers. Even the publisher of the *Mirror,* Poe's old enemy, urged admirers to come to his rescue. To save his pride, Poe responded that his financial condition was not good but that he was hardly starving—though in truth he nearly was. To one editor Poe wrote: "That, as the inevitable consequence of so long an illness, I have been in want of money, it would be folly in me to deny—but that I have ever materially suffered from privation, beyond the extent of my capacity for suffering, is not altogether true. That I am 'without friends' is a gross calumny."

Virginia's death left Poe and Virginia's mother, Maria, inconsolable. Friends gathered to try to help them through their grief. One friend who came to console the grieving widower was Marie Louise "Loui" Shew. Exactly Virginia's age, the two had become friends when the Poes lived in Greenwich Village. Loui became a frequent visitor to the cottage in Fordham where Virginia lay dying. She was also a great comfort to Poe and Maria after Virginia's death. Loui came by the cottage three or four times a week to minister to Poe, who was suffering from anxiety and the still undiagnosed illness.

Loui supervised Poe's diet and exercise. She did all she could to keep his nervousness in check and to provide him with a stable environment. It happened that just a few days after Virginia's funeral Poe came into several hundred dollars as the result of a favorable verdict in his libel suit against Thomas Dunn English. This money, combined with the money that came in the form of donations during Virginia's illness, enabled Poe and Maria to live a much more comfortable life. But the "Literati" sketches had not been forgotten and Poe was still a marked man to many in the literary world. When word began to circulate that he was dressed in new clothes and serving fine foods at his table, his enemies accused him of misusing the funds raised for Virginia's care. Poe was too sick to respond. He lay in bed, ministered to by Loui, both of them convinced he was going to die.

It took Poe several months to recover, somewhat, from Virginia's death. Later, he told a friend that his wife's death had actually provided him with a release from the torture of her suffering. He said during the years of her illness, "I became insane," a period interrupted by "long intervals of horrible sanity." His drinking, he said, was his attempt to maintain that sanity. As he wrote to a friend, Poe believed his "enemies preferred the insanity to the drink rather than the drink to the insanity." Poe's argument is suspect, not just because he confided to Maria that "I was never *really* insane, except on occasions where my heart was touched," but because he often fell back into drinking even after Virginia died. However, he did seem to be convinced that her death left him finally free to take stock of his own pain.

His poem "Ulalume" (1847), written not long after Virginia's death, is narrated by a man who is consumed by the memory of his dead wife and yet, at times, almost able to forget she ever existed. The poem suggests that memory can both haunt and heal. But, in a darker turn, the poem also implies that the entire universe is subject to death, not just its lowly human inhabitants. This marks a development in Poe's thinking—in "The Conqueror Worm" he implied that the gods watch, impassively, as each man lives out his little life. In "Ulalume" he now proposed that even gods, planets, and stars would also someday die.

Poe's new obsession with the stars kept him out on his porch, gazing into the night sky for hours at a time. He began work on a lecture called "The Universe" which became the basis for a book he entitled *Eureka: A Prose Poem.* Poe's subject was the creation of the cosmos.

Though he had no formal training in science or astronomy, Poe took it upon himself to explain how he thought the universe had been created. He theorized that a divine being burst open the universe into atoms that, in their inevitable will to regroup, came together to form rotating solar systems. In a natural reaction to the force that had propelled them apart, these systems would eventually come back together, and, in essence, form God. He suggested that this process would occur over and over again, its rhythm symbolizing the heartbeat of the divine.

Poe was convinced that he had revealed the very origins of the universe, as well as the nature of God. He felt that each human soul was part of God and that therefore each human being was God. By that logic he came, perhaps inevitably, to the conclusion that he, Poe, was God. This outraged those who were certain God was a supreme deity distinct from and superior to man. Loui Shew, in particular, was so upset by Poe's assertions that she ended their friendship. Poe felt she was abandoning him. He wrote to Maria in a depressed moment: "I must die. I have no desire to live since I have done *Eureka*. I could accomplish nothing more."

Though he had suffered because of his love for Virginia, having felt so keenly the pain of her illness, Poe seemed to know how her influence had steadied him. With Loui Shew out of his life, Poe set about looking for a replacement. He was hoping to make a good marriage. He saw this as his only way of permanently pulling himself out of wretched poverty. As he appeared to be washed up in so many New York literary circles, he set his sights on women in other cities.

Poe used this picture, made in 1847, as a visiting card. Known as *cartes de visites,* these photographic calling cards were wildly popular in the middle of the nineteenth century.

These included the poet Jane Locke, with whom Poe had a torrid correspondence. After several months of exchanging letters, in which Poe tried delicately to inquire about her marital status, he visited her home in Lowell, Massachusetts. After discovering that Jane was in her forties and had a husband and several children, he promptly transferred his affections to a relative of hers, Nancy "Annie" Richmond. Annie also had a husband, but she and Poe carried on a romantic friendship. At first, Annie's husband did not take Poe very seriously or see him as any kind of threat, until it occurred to him that Poe was becoming far too passionate about his wife and vice versa. He quickly took steps to force the lovers apart.

Realizing that marrying Annie would be impossible, Poe sought her counsel as to his relationship with yet another woman, Sarah Helen Whitman.

Helen Whitman lived in Providence, Rhode Island and was a sophisticated, well-educated, and attractive woman. A leading American critic as well as a poet, Helen had read Poe's stories and found them shocking— and utterly fascinating. The two had never met, so Helen pursued Poe with poetry and he responded in kind. They exchanged unsigned pieces and confided their interest in mutual friends, but neither dared speak directly to the other. In the meantime, Poe had gone back to Richmond, Virginia to visit his sister and other friends. While there, he had encountered Elmira Royster, now the widow Elmira Shelton, the woman he had loved and lost when he was seventeen. Her father had kept them apart, but now they were reunited. Their relationship was quickly rekindled and Poe was on the verge of proposing marriage to her when he received a promising poem in the mail from Helen. He dropped everything and hurried north.

In September of 1848, Poe arrived at Helen's home in Providence, where she lived with her mother and fragile younger sister, Anna. Widowed at twenty-nine, Helen had never remarried because she felt obligated to care for her family. She was now forty-five, six years older than Poe. During his time in Rhode Island, Poe wooed Helen relentlessly and proposed to her after only two days. "Your hand rested within mine," he wrote her, "and my whole soul shook with a tremulous ecstasy."

Although Helen was intrigued by Poe and flattered by his interest, she had her doubts about him as a potential husband. She knew his reputation, and many of her Boston friends spoke of him with anger. She also heard stories about his drinking, though Poe vigorously defended himself. "I swear to you that my soul is incapable of dishonor," Poe wrote Helen, "that, with the exception of occasional follies and excesses which I bitterly lament, but to which I have been driven by intolerable sorrow, and which are hourly committed by others without attracting any notice whatever—I can call to mind no act of my life which would bring a blush to my cheek—or to yours."

Poe wrote Helen countless letters, begging her to marry him. She responded that she was too old, too unattractive, too ill. He wrote back immediately, swearing theirs would be a union of two loving, like-minded spirits and that age, health, and beauty did not matter. The flurry of proposals and counter-proposals continued for a month, then Poe could stand it no longer and swore he would never propose to her again.

Even as Poe was declaring his love for Helen, he resumed his courtship of Annie Richmond. Annie's husband, Charles, invited Poe to stay with them and Poe accepted—then used his proximity to woo his host's wife. Helen's hesitations did not accord with Poe's passionate romantic nature, and he soon convinced himself that it was Annie he truly needed at his side for his ultimate happiness. Charles tolerated Poe's affections because he was certain they were not serious. Charles, like many of Poe's friends, took the cynical view that Poe seemed to prefer women who were not free to marry over those who were—they speculated that Poe's professed desire to marry was in fact countered by an even more overwhelming desire not to marry. Poe was more in love with the idea of love than the reality of it.

Helen may have loved Poe and wanted to marry him, but she was a genteel, conventional soul at heart. Poe was a wild bohemian without a dime to his name. She sent an ambiguous letter to him at Annie Richmond's house, suggesting that perhaps their relationship had no future, whereupon Poe fled to Boston and tried to commit suicide by swallowing a large dose of laudanum. The drug, a derivative of opium, made him very sick but did not kill him. For two days, he stumbled around the city, incoherent and violently ill. He was finally able to collect himself enough to get to Providence, where he and Helen

Edgar Allan Poe, photographed at a time when he was visibly distraught. *(The Library of Congress.)*

engaged in an emotionally charged altercation that lasted for several days. She was terrified by his appearance and mental state, while he alternately begged her to marry him then renounced her forever. Somehow, during this time, Poe had his picture taken. In it, the circles under his eyes are darker than ever. One side of his face is swollen and his entire visage appears to be off-kilter.

After several meetings and dramatic confrontations—Helen's family had to summon a doctor to attend to Poe at one point—Helen finally agreed to marry Poe on two conditions. The first was that he give up drinking, and the second that her mother approve of the union. Deep down, Helen must have known that neither condition could be met. Although a notice of their upcoming wedding was published in several newspapers, their engagement was over almost before the ink was dry. Someone reported to Helen that Poe had been seen drinking and a confrontation ensued. Although neither Poe nor Helen formally called off the marriage, when Poe left Providence their relationship was over. Poe vowed he would have no more to do with literary women.

Poe's courtship of Helen had lasted several exhausting months, during which time he wrote little. Back in New York, alone once more and determined to try to salvage the dregs of his literary career, he took on any assignment that might earn him a little money. He became a correspondent for a Pottsville, Pennsylvania paper called the *Miner's Journal*. He also wrote for a paper called *Flag of the Union,* which he felt was tasteless and common but which nonetheless paid well.

He went back on the lecture circuit, using his talks to elaborate on the ideas he laid out in one of his most famous pieces of nonfiction, an essay about poetry called "The Poetic Principle." In this essay, Poe explains that poetry has its origins in humankind's need for truth and beauty, and that a poem need have no other reason for existence than the aesthetic pleasure it gives the reader or listener. This essay stands today as a major event in the history of literary criticism. In it Poe coined many of the terms and beliefs that have become commonplace when talking about writing, but he also took a strong stand against the traditional beliefs about writing poetry. Using examples of his favorite poems, Poe carefully and thoroughly constructed an argument explaining what made good poetry. "The Poetic Principle," which is nearly seven thousand words long, shows Poe's analytical eye and acute attention to detail. Much as he delighted in solving cryptograms, Poe also enjoyed puzzling out the mysteries of poetry.

Even as Poe was writing some of his most powerful and lasting works, including the poems "Annabel Lee" (1849) and "The Bells" (1849), he was still barely able to keep himself fed and clothed. He continued to borrow money at every turn. A young writer and editor from Illinois, Edward Patterson, admired Poe and wrote to him suggesting they work together to publish the magazine Poe had always dreamed of, but the idea would never be realized.

Still, Poe went on a lecture tour to try to raise money for the magazine he wanted so desperately, but trouble continued to plague him. In Philadelphia, he went on another drinking spree—which he later swore to Maria was a mild case of cholera—and was arrested and briefly jailed. In jail, he suffered badly from symptoms of the withdrawal from alcohol. When he was released, he found he had lost the briefcase containing all his lecture notes. He became paranoid and increasingly delusional. Hoping to borrow money from a friend, Poe appeared on the man's doorstep disheveled and missing a shoe.

Poe finally made his way back to Richmond, Virginia. He still hoped to find investors for his magazine among the friends he had there. He also hoped to earn a little money he could send to Maria—he felt terrible that he was so much of the time unable to provide for her.

The incoherent drunk who left Philadelphia became a sober, neatly dressed man of letters in the familiar environs of Richmond. Poe managed to deliver several versions of his lecture on poetics and was very well received by the city. He took the time to once again become reacquainted with Elmira Royster, the woman he had loved as a boy and almost proposed to the year before. It was not long before Poe was planning to propose again, waging a romantic campaign that was every bit as intense as his courtship of Helen Whitman had been. Elmira shared Helen's concern about Poe's drinking, so he joined an anti-drinking group called the Sons of Temperance and pledged that alcohol would never again pass his lips.

Elmira's late husband had written a clause in his will saying that if she remarried, she would have to give up a

A letter from Poe to his aunt Maria, 1849. *(Fales Library, New York University.)*

Elmira Shelton, the woman Poe loved as a boy then rediscovered years later. *(The Valentine Museum, Richmond, Virginia.)*

substantial portion of her inheritance. Despite this, it seems as though Elmira was won over by Poe's courtship, and planned to accept his proposal. But he never got a chance to make it. While on his way north again to collect Maria and bring her to live with him in Richmond, Poe got off the train when it stopped in Baltimore on September 27, 1849 and disappeared.

There have been several theories as to what happened to Poe during the week that he was missing. At first, there was the belief that he had been a victim of "cooping." This was the practice of literally dragging men off the street, keeping them drunk, and forcing them to vote at different districts during an election. As Baltimore was having an election at the time, this theory seemed plausible for many years.

Another theory is that Elmira Shelton's brothers were convinced Poe was a gold digger and would be a poor choice for their sister. According to this theory, they followed Poe north and administered a serious beating to keep him from returning to Richmond.

The most likely explanation is that Poe ran into some old friends from West Point in Baltimore and went off on a binge as he had done previously in New York and Philadelphia. No one knows for sure what happened to Poe during those six days, but on October 3, 1849, he was found in the gutter outside a Baltimore tavern, disheveled and barely conscious. He was taken to a hospital at the Washington Medical College. His symptoms included the "D.T.s"—or delirium tremens— a condition that causes hallucinations and afflicts many alcoholics during withdrawal. There was the added complication of encephalitis, an inflammation of the brain that can be caused by exposure to extremely cold weather.

Poe spent several days in the hospital before lapsing into a coma and dying on Sunday, October 7, 1849. A witness reported that his final words were "Lord help my poor soul." He was buried the following day. Because news of his death had not yet traveled far, there were few mourners at the funeral. A devastated Maria had to read the news in the paper, then write to friends in Baltimore to find out if it was true. Maria lived another twenty-two years but never quite recovered from all of her personal losses over the years, including the loss of the man she had come to think of as a son.

Poe's poor judgement haunted him even after his death. Before he died, he had appointed Rufus Griswold to oversee any posthumous publication of his work. Griswold was a miserable choice, as he and Poe had always disliked each other. As Griswold said, "I was not his friend, nor was he mine." Though Griswold did make sure collections of Poe's work were published, he managed to wreak havoc on his reputation. He published several essays bemoaning Poe's lack of character and his dissolute ways. He made Poe out to be an immoral drunkard not worth the time it took to read him. Poe's few friends tried to rebut Griswold's claims, but to little avail.

Griswold's smear campaign was initially successful, but Poe eventually became an object of fascination precisely because of the air of scandal attached to his name. Particularly in France, where the poet Charles Baudelaire devoted himself to translating Poe's works, he was soon much more popular than he had ever been during his lifetime. Baudelaire inaugurated the school of symbolism in French poetry, largely based on his experiences reading Poe. Baudelaire's translations stand as some of the best ever done, as well as some of the most important of his own works—he devoted much of his creative energies to reading and interpreting the man he saw as his own double.

Thanks to Baudelaire, Poe was soon considered fashionable throughout Europe. A host of great thinkers and writers since have paid him compliments and acknowledged his influence on their work. These include Friedrich Nietzsche, Rainer Maria Rilke, Franz Kafka, William Butler Yeats, Thomas Hardy, George Bernard Shaw, Fyodor Dostoevsky, Arthur Rimbaud, Walter Pater, Oscar Wilde, Robert Louis Stevenson, Rudyard Kipling, Joseph Conrad, Vladimir Nabokov, and James Joyce. British novelist D. H. Lawrence wrote a lengthy essay full of admiration in which he explained the importance and great value of Poe's work. Modernist poet T. S. Eliot could never bring himself to say Poe was a great writer, but he would not deny Poe's importance.

At least one author in particular owes Poe an enormous debt. Arthur Conan Doyle, who wrote detective stories featuring his well-known hero, Sherlock Holmes, freely admitted to modeling Holmes on Poe's Dupin— even allowing other characters to suggest to Holmes that he is reminiscent of Dupin. Conan Doyle's hero lived in a world created by Edgar Allan Poe—he could hardly have existed without Dupin's precedence.

American writers, including Nathaniel Hawthorne, Herman Melville, F. Scott Fitzgerald, and Thomas Wolfe, all paid homage to Poe in their writings. He came to represent for them an original American voice. Today, the Mystery Writers of America call their annual awards the "Edgars" after Poe.

But Poe's legacy has a darker side, too. His life, and especially Griswold's interpretation of it, gave further credence to the theory that artists must suffer for their art—that writers must know depravation and fear if they are to be able to write about those things. Poe never wrote while drunk, and his drinking, in fact, brought an early end to both his career and his life. But later readers have often valorized the image of Poe as a devil-may-care bon vivant. They imagined that Poe's alcoholism was the fuel for his talent rather than what smothered it. Similarly, Poe's contentious relationship with his critics and with other writers came to symbolize the idea of the true artist as an outsider, one who might not be understood or appreciated properly in his own lifetime but who would be rewarded after his death. It is the final irony of Poe's life that the circumstances he resented most—his poverty, his inability to fit in, his trouble keeping work, and his drinking—became the very things that made him a hero to future generations.

The flip side of this legacy is that Poe was immensely dedicated to his craft. In his short life, he brought imagination, insight, and hard work to the developing field of American letters, and left that field forever changed.

Major Works

Poems
"Tamerlane" 1827
"Al Aaraaf" 1829
"Lenore" 1831
"The City in the Sea" 1831
"The Conqueror Worm" 1838
"The Haunted Palace" 1839
"The Raven" 1845
"Ulalume" 1847
"Annabel Lee" 1849
"The Bells" 1849
"Alone" 1849

Stories
"Berenice" 1835
"Morella" 1835
"The Unparalleled Adventure of One Hans Pfaall" 1835
"Ligeia" 1838
"The Fall of the House of Usher" 1839
"William Wilson" 1839
"The Murders in the Rue Morgue" 1841

"The Oval Portrait" 1842
"The Masque of the Red Death" 1842
"The Mystery of Marie Roget" 1843
"The Tell-Tale Heart" 1843
"The Gold-Bug" 1843
"The Pit and the Pendulum" 1843
"The Black Cat" 1843
"The Spectacles" 1844
"The Premature Burial" 1844
"The Purloined Letter" 1845
"The System of Doctor Tarr and Professor Fether" 1845
"The Facts in the Case of M. Valdemar" 1845
"The Cask of Amontillado" 1846
"Hop-Frog" 1849

Longer works
The Narrative of Arthur Gordon Pym of Nantucket 1838
Eureka: A Prose Poem 1848

Essays
"The Philosophy of Composition" 1846
"The Poetic Principle" 1848

Timeline

1809   Born in Boston on January 19 to David and Eliza (Arnold) Poe; moves with family to New York City six months later; soon after, Poe's father abandons his family for good.

1811   Poe's mother dies on December 8; Edgar, separated from his siblings, goes to live with John and Frances Allan.

1815   Moves to England with the Allans.

1820   The Allans and Edgar return to Virginia.

1826   Edgar begins studies at the University of Virginia.

1827   Enlists in the army; publishes *Tamerlane and Other Poems.*

1829   Frances Allan dies; "Al Aaraaf" is published.

1830   Poe enters West Point Military Academy.

1831   Is court-martialed out of West Point.

1834   John Allan dies; Poe is cut out of his estate entirely.

1835   Poe goes to work for the *Southern Literary Messenger.*

1836   Marries his cousin Virginia Clemm.

1838   *The Narrative of Arthur Gordon Pym of Nantucket* is published; Poe goes to Philadelphia.

1839   "The Fall of the House of Usher" and "William Wilson" are published; *Tales of the Grotesque and Arabesque* is published.

1841   "The Murders in the Rue Morgue" is published, with it, Poe invents the detective story.
1842   "The Masque of the Red Death" is published.
1843   "The Pit and the Pendulum" is published.
1844   Poe moves to New York.
1845   "The Raven" is published to great acclaim; Poe becomes sole proprietor of the *Broadway Journal*.
1846   The *Journal* goes out of business; Poe moves to Fordham.
1847   Virginia Poe dies.
1848   *Eureka* is published; Poe proposes to Helen Whitman.
1849   "Hop-Frog" is published; in Richmond, Poe proposes to Elmira Royster Shelton. He dies on October 7.

Sources

CHAPTER TWO: Battle of Wills

p. 26, "I call God to witness . . ." Edgar Allan Poe, *The Letters of Edgar Allan Poe,* Volume I, John Ward Ostrom, ed., (NY: Gordian Press, Inc., 1966), 41.

p. 29, "My determination . . ." Ibid., 7.

p. 29, "You take delight in exposing me . . ." Ibid., 8.

CHAPTER THREE: West Point

p. 40, "The time in which I . . ." Poe, *The Letters,* Vol. I, 41-42.

p. 41, "From the time of this writing . . ." Ibid., 42.

CHAPTER FOUR: "Muddy" and Virginia

p. 44, "attending her [mother] . . ." Poe, *The Letters,* Vol. I, 67.

p. 45, "I am perishing . . ." Ibid., 50.

p. 46, "Brought up to no profession . . ." Ibid., 68.

p. 49, "Are you sure Virginia . . ." Ibid., 71.

p. 50, "What have I *to live for?* . . ." Ibid., 70.

CHAPTER FIVE: Hatchet Man

p. 54, "too purely imbecile . . ." Jeffrey Meyers, *Edgar Allan Poe: His Life and Legacy* (NY: Charles Scribner's Sons, 1992), 83.

p. 59, "while I resided in Richmond . . ." Poe, *The Letters,* Volume I, 156.

p. 64, "blood-red" Edgar Allan Poe, *Complete Tales and Poems* (NY: Vintage Books, 1975), 659.

p. 64, "That the play . . ." Ibid.

CHAPTER SIX: Washington Follies

p. 66, "*even a word or two . . .*" Kenneth Silverman, *Edgar A. Poe* (NY: Harper Collins Publishers, 1991), 146.

p. 76, "In my last great disappointment..." Poe, *The Letters,* Vol. II, 318.

p. 79, "Literature is the most noble . . ." Ibid., 427.

CHAPTER SEVEN: Broadway Journal

p. 82, "excessively slothful, and . . ." Poe, *The Letters,* Vol. I, 256.

p. 93, "I have need of the most . . ." Ibid., 301.

CHAPTER EIGHT: "Lord Help My Poor Soul"

p. 97, "become deranged" Silverman, *Edgar A. Poe,* 301.

p. 99, "Mr. Briggs has never composed . . ." Ibid., 307.

p. 100, "his tongue shows itself . . ." Meyers, *Edgar Allan Poe,* 196.

p. 101, "That, as the inevitable consequence . . ." Poe, *The Letters,* Vol. II, 338.

p. 103, "I became insane . . ." Silverman, *Edgar A. Poe,* 334.

p. 103, "enemies preferred the insanity . . ." Poe, *The Letters,* Vol. II,   356.

p. 103, "I was never *really* insane . . ." Ibid., 452.

p. 104, "I must die . . ." Ibid., 452.

p. 107, "Your hand rested . . ." Ibid., 387.

p. 107, "I swear to you . . ." Ibid., 393.

p. 115, "Lord help my poor soul." Meyers, *Edgar Allan Poe,* 255.

p. 116, "I was not his friend . . ." Ibid., 262.

Bibliography

Allen, H. Israfel. *The Life and Times of Edgar Allan Poe.* New York: Farrar, 1934.

Poe, Edgar Allan. *Complete Tales and Poems.* New York: Vintage Books, 1975.

————. *Letters of Edgar Allan Poe,* Vols. I and II. Edited by John Ward Ostrom. New York: Gordian Press, 1966.

————. *The Portable Poe: Stories, Poems, Non-Fiction, and Correspondence.* Edited by Philip Van Doren Stern. New York: Penguin, 1973.

Schoell, William. "The Life and Times of Edgar Allan Poe." *Macabre.* October, 1987.

————. "The Horrific Tradition of Edgar Allan Poe." *Macabre.* November, 1990.

————. *Remarkable Journeys: The Story of Jules Verne.* Greensboro, NC: Morgan Reynolds, 2002.

Silverman, Kenneth. *Edgar A. Poe: Mournful and Never-ending Remembrance.* New York: HarperCollins, 1991.

Thomas, Dwight D., and David K. Jacobson. *The Poe Log: A Documentary Life of Edgar Allan Poe.* Boston: G.K. Hall, 1987.

Thompson, Gary Richard. *Edgar Allan Poe: Essays and Reviews.* New York: Viking Press, 1984.

Walsh, John Evangelist. *Midnight Dreary: The Mysterious Death of Edgar Allan Poe.* New Brunswick: Rutgers University Press, 1998.

Index